Make Way for Lucia

A comedy

John van Druten
Based on the novels by E. F. Benson

Samuel French — London
New York - Toronto - Hollywood

MAKE WAY FOR LUCIA

Produced by The Theatre Guild at the Cort Theatre, New York City, on 22nd December 1948, with the following cast:

Major Benjamin Flint	Philip Tonge
Grosvenor	Cherry Hardy
Miss Mapp	Catherine Willard
Georgie Pillson	Cyril Ritchard
Mrs Emmeline Lucas (Lucia)	Isabel Jeans
Mr Wyse	Ivan Simpson
Mrs Wyse	Essex Dane
Rev. Kenneth Bartlett	Guy Spaull
Mrs Bartlett	Doreen Lang
Godiva Plaistow	Viola Roache
Signor Cortese	Kurt Kasznar

Directed by Mr van Druten
Produced by Theresa Helburn and Lawrence Langner

COPYRIGHT INFORMATION

(See also page ii)

MAKE WAY FOR LUCIA

The professional British première of the play was in 1995 in a touring production with the following cast of characters:

Major Benjamin Flint	John Nettleton
Grosvenor	Lavinia Bertram
Miss Mapp	Marcia Warren
Georgie Pillson	John Wells
Mrs Emmeline Lucas (Lucia)	Angela Thorne
Mr Wyse	David Crosse
Mrs Wyse	Jill Johnson
Rev. Kenneth Bartlett	Brian Hewlett
Mrs Bartlett	Deddie Davies
Godiva Plaistow	Antonia Pemberton
Signor Cortese	Dominic Borrelli

Directed by Alan Strachan
Designed by Paul Farnsworth
Lighting by Leonard Tucker

CHARACTERS

Major Benjy Flint. A soldier-like, huffing, puffing man of about 50.

Grosvenor. A very correct parlour-maid of about 35.

Miss Mapp. A somewhat aggressive woman in her early 40s, built on a rather generous scale. Her two principal emotions are curiosity and resentment. When she is not being offended, her manner is genial — too genial — and inclined to be arch.

Georgie Pillson. Anywhere from 38 to 45; plumpish and rather nice-looking; inclined to be easily fussed or upset. His hair is auburn, with a strong suspicion of being dyed and also of being partly a toupee. He is pleasant and likeable, and must not be exaggerated into anything approaching a caricature.

Mrs Emmeline Lucas (Lucia). She is about 40. A good-looking woman, she is something of a phoney, but never to herself. She believes wholeheartedly in all her poses and acts, and perhaps the best clue to her is that she is quite violently in love with herself. Her manner combines gush and artificiality, with a considerable amount of practical shrewdness and a capacity for quite ruthless drive. She has a great, if very slightly condescending, charm with anyone who will pay court to her. Her attitude to Georgie is a trifle proprietory, but warmly affectionate, and at moments, almost motherly. Her affection for him is perhaps the only real thing about her.

Mr Wyse. He is a courtly gentleman with silver hair. He has a habit of bowing slightly to anyone he addresses, or whose name he mentions.

Mrs Wyse. She is a portly old lady.

Rev. Kenneth Bartlett. He is of the hearty and jocular type, about 45. He talks always in broad, vaudeville Scots.

Mrs Bartlett. She is a tiny, mouselike woman who speaks very seldom and then in squeaks.

Godiva Plaistow. She is a short, roly-poly woman of 50. She is a breathless type, talking mainly in short, rather telegraphic sentences.

Signor Cortese. He is a florid Italian with Caruso moustache.

CHARACTERS

Major Benjamin Flint
Grosvenor
Miss Mapp
George Pillson
Mrs Emmeline Lucas (Lucia)
Mr Wyse
Mrs Wyse
Rev. Kenneth Bartlett
Mrs Bartlett
Godiva Plaistow
Signor Cortese

The action of the play takes place in the drawing-room of a house in Tilling, a small town in the South of England, during July, August and September

ACT I
SCENE 1. Morning. July
SCENE 2. Morning. Four weeks later

ACT II
SCENE 1. Afternoon. Two weeks later
SCENE 2. Afternoon. Ten days later
SCENE 3. Evening. A week later

ACT III
SCENE 1. Morning. The next day
SCENE 2. Evening. The same day

Also by John van Druten published by Samuel French Ltd

I Remember Mama

ACT I
Scene 1

Morning Scene

The drawing-room of a house in Tilling, a small town in the South of England. A morning in July

The room is an attractive one, with Edwardian decoration: white paint and summer chintzes. In the R wall are two french windows leading on to a garden. Flanking the downstage window are two pedestals with vases of summer flowers upon them. The long curtains are lavender. There is a wall light bracket just below the upstage french window and a canvas on an easel stands in front of the windows

There is a three-walled recess UR. On the R wall of this recess is a fireplace. On the wall over the fireplace is a portrait and on the wall just below the fireplace is a bell pull. Light brackets flank the fireplace. On the rear wall of the recess is the door to the dining-room and the upstairs parts of the house. Just left of this door is a round table with an urn of greenery upon it. On the rear wall are miniature and other pictures (bad ones, all) for dressing. In the L wall of the recess is a built-in bookcase. There is a light-bracket on the rear wall. Just below the bookcase is a supporting pillar running to the ceiling

In the recess are a piano and piano bench, with keyboard facing upstage. There is room on both sides of the piano for actors to pass. Below the piano is a large sofa, running straight across the stage. At the L end of the sofa is a round side table. To the R of the sofa, and midway between it and the downstage french window, is a small armchair, upholstered in yellow. Upstage of this chair is a small side table

In the UL wall is a curtained arch with a two-step rise. This arch opens into the front hall, which leads off L to the outside and off R to the kitchen and other parts of the house. There is a chandelier hanging in the hall. In front of the wall spaces to R and L of this arch are two identical cabinets for holding bric-a-brac, books, etc. To the R of the R cabinet is a straight chair upholstered in lavender

Upstage in the L wall is a large bay window, looking out on to the village street. The curtains here are flowered and busy chintz and match the covering

on the sofa. Facing into the window is a desk with desk chair in the kneehole.
Downstage in the L wall is a fireplace. Over the mantel is a flowered print,
and on the mantel are ornaments and gewgaws. Near the fireplace, and
facing on stage at an angle, is a love-seat upholstered in a purplish velour.
In front of the downstage corner of the fireplace is a pouffe covered with
material matching the L window curtains and sofa. There are light brackets
flanking the fireplace and one above the large bay window L

The CURTAIN *rises on an empty stage. A bell sounds off* UL

Grosvenor enters through the arch R and exits L

Major (*off* UL) Is Mrs Lucas at home?
Grosvenor (*off* UL) No, sir, I'm afraid she isn't.
Major (*off* UL) Is she likely to be long, do you know?
Grosvenor (*off* UL) I don't think so, sir. Would you care to come in and wait?
Major (*off* UL) Thanks.

Grosvenor and the Major enter through the arch. He carries a bound copy
of his "Indian Diaries" manuscript

Grosvenor If you'll just take a seat in here, sir. I'm sure Mrs Lucas won't
be long.
Major Thanks. It's Major Flint, tell her.
Grosvenor Yes, sir.

Grosvenor exits through arch to R

The Major goes to the love-seat, puts down the manuscript, picks up a copy
of Dante's Inferno, *opens it, and sits on the love-seat. As he starts to read it,*
Mapp is heard off UL

Mapp (*off* UL) Is anyone in? It's Miss Mapp.

The Major puts the Dante on the love-seat, picks up the manuscript, and
hurriedly goes towards the french windows R, to make an escape

Mapp enters through the arch from L

Why, Major Benjy!
Major (*pretending surprise*) Oh, morning, Liz.
Mapp What are *you* doing here?
Major (*too airily*) Oh, just paying a call, you know.

Mapp But *I* don't *live* here any more, Major. Not for the rest of the summer.

Major (*going to Mapp*) Yes, I know, but — well, as a matter of fact, I wasn't calling on *you*, girlie. Calling on the new arrival. On your tenant, Mrs Lucas.

Mapp Calling at *this* hour of the morning?

Major Well, I paid my respects yesterday afternoon. And … I was telling Mrs Lucas about my Indian army experiences, and she was kind enough to say that she'd be interested to read some of my old diaries. (*He holds up the manuscript*) Highly intelligent woman.

Mapp Because she was interested in your diaries?

Major Now, wait a minute. Halt the ride. Halt the ride. Don't start getting jealous.

Mapp Jealous? Well, really Major! I suppose — (*she sits on the sofa*) I suppose all those little bits of Italian that she drops into her conversation — I suppose *those* impressed you, too?

Major Now, where's the harm in a woman being able to talk Italian?

Mapp No harm, Major, *if* she can.

Major (*going to the love-seat*) Got a copy of Dante's *Inferno* lying over here. (*He picks up the Dante from the love-seat and goes back to* C)

Mapp Pure affectation. (*She goes to the easel*) Like everything else about her. (*Pointing to the canvas on the easel*) Her painting — (*Going to the piano, pointing to it*) Her music. No, Major, I'm afraid your Mrs Lucas is a fake — a *poseuse*, from head to toe.

Major Now, really! (*He tosses Dante on to the side table*)

Mapp Her clothes, too. You should see the outfit she's gone shopping in this morning. In our little High Street! By the way, who else was here when you called on her yesterday?

Major Well, Mr and Mrs Wyse ——

Mapp Oh, she's got hold of *them* already, has she? Who else?

Major Only that red-haired fellow who seems to be travelling with her. Staying at the hotel here. Millson ——

Mapp Oh, Mr *Pillson*, yes. (*She goes to the desk, picks up the letters and postcards, and leafs through them*) He was always dancing attendance on her in Riseholme. That's where they come from, you know. I met them there last year when I was visiting in Warwickshire.

Major Pillson, eh? Now, there's a fellow I can't take to.

Mapp Oh, I thought him charming. (*She starts to read the mail*)

Major Seemed to me more like an old maid than a man. (*He notices Mapp*) I say, aren't those *her* letters, Liz?

Mapp That's what I was looking to see. (*Reading the addresses*) "Lucas — Lucas — Mrs *Emmeline* Lucas." So *that's* her real name, is it? (*She turns over a postcard to read the message*)

Major I say, Liz, you can't ——

Mapp (*turning; facing him down*) *What* can't I, Major?
Major (*cowed*) Oh, nothing, nothing. None of my business, I suppose. Well,
if *you*'re staying, Liz, I think I'll come back later. (*He starts for the arch*)
Mapp When you can find her *alone*?
Major What?
Mapp (*going to the Major*) But just a word of warning, Major. I rather
suspect that Mrs Lucas intends to try and *take over* our little town of Tilling.
I think you should be careful not to get roped in.
Major No, no, you're wrong there, Liz. She told me yesterday that *peace* and
quiet were what she'd come here for.
Mapp And I suppose you believed her?
Major Why? Don't *you*? What makes you think —— ?
Mapp It's all right, Major, it's all right. Run along.
Major (*disturbed*) I say, you're not offended about anything, are you?
Mapp (*coldly*) No, no, of course not. Run along.
Major Really, I don't understand women!

The Major exits through the arch to L

Mapp goes back to reading the postcard

Grosvenor enters UR, *carrying a vase of flowers*

*Grosvenor makes a slight sound upon seeing what Mapp is doing. Mapp
turns at the sound and puts the mail on the desk as Grosvenor places the vase
on the side table by the sofa*

Mapp Oh, good-morning, Grosvenor. I just popped in to see if Mrs Lucas
was happy in my little house. (*She goes to the arch*) There have been one
or two little changes here, I notice. A new piano. I really don't know why.
Mine was always considered a very fine instrument. It belonged to my
mother. (*Pointing to a portrait on wall* L *of the arch*) *That* was my mother.
Grosvenor Indeed, miss?
Mapp (*going to the love-seat*) And one or two pieces of furniture missing.
I suppose Mrs Lucas put them away?
Grosvenor (*moving on line with Mapp*) Yes, miss. They're upstairs in the
attic.
Mapp I think perhaps I'll just *run* upstairs if I may. There was a hot-water-
bottle that I seem to have forgotten to take with me. (*She moves up a step*)
Grosvenor (*moving up with Mapp*) I'll be glad to get it for you, miss, if you'll
tell me where it is.
Mapp Well, that's the silly thing. I can't quite remember. But if I just *rootle*
— (*She moves up a step*)

Grosvenor (*moving up with Mapp*) I'll come *with* you, miss.

Mapp Oh, there's no need for *you* to trouble yourself. (*She moves up a step*)

Grosvenor (*moving up with Mapp*) It's no trouble, miss.

Mapp (*defeated*) Well, perhaps some other time, then. (*She goes to the piano and inspects the music lying there*) You've been with Mrs Lucas a long time, haven't you?

Grosvenor Fifteen years, miss.

Mapp She and Mr Pillson are great friends, aren't they?

Grosvenor Mr Pillson has always been a friend of the family, miss.

Mapp Yes, but I mean — since *Mr* Lucas' *death*, I expect Mr Pillson has been very attentive. Mrs Lucas is far too young and attractive to remain a *widow* long, don't you think?

Grosvenor (*coldly*) I couldn't say, miss, I'm sure.

The bell sounds off UL

Excuse me, miss. There's the bell.

Grosvenor exits through the arch to L

Mapp goes to the arch and listens to hear who is calling

Georgie (*off* UL) Good-morning, Grosvenor. Mrs Lucas at home?

Grosvenor (*off* UL) No, Mr Pillson. But I don't think she'll be long.

Mapp moves to the sofa and reverses two cushions from the brown to the yellow side

Georgie (*off* UL) Oh. Well, then, I'll come in and wait.

Grosvenor (*off* UL) Miss Mapp is in the drawing-room, sir. The lady the house belongs to.

Georgie (*off* UL) Oh?

Georgie enters through the arch from L

Good-morning.

Grosvenor crosses the arch to exit R

Mapp Mr Pillson, I'm Miss Mapp.

Georgie Of course.

Mapp We met once at Riseholme, when I was visiting there last year.

Georgie Of course I remember. (*He shakes hands with Mapp, a high and formal handshake*) How do you do.

Mapp (*sitting on the* R *end of the sofa*) And how is dear Riseholme? Such a sweet town. So Elizabethan.

Georgie (*sitting on* L *arm of the sofa*) Well, it's still Elizabethan.

Mapp And all those charming people I met. Those two dear girls who were so nice to me. Goosie and ——

Georgie (*effusively*) Oh ... Goosie and Piggy Antrobus. Two of my dearest friends.

Mapp I expect they're all going to miss Mrs Lucas dreadfully. I wonder she was able to tear herself away. What *did* make her decide to leave, and come to *us*, do you know?

Georgie (*sitting on the sofa*) No, I don't really. I've wondered about it, too. She merely said she wanted a little peace and quiet. Though that's not *like* Lucia.

Mapp By the way, that name — Lucia. Where does it come from?

Georgie It's Italian. Lucia, the wife of Lucas.

Mapp Oh, yes, she's quite an Italian scholar, isn't she? You speak it, too, don't you? I remember hearing you talk it together?

Georgie Yes, it's one of the sort of games we play — like baby-talk.

Mapp I'm sure you'll miss her, too. Such devoted friends you've always been.

Georgie (*rising*) Well, as a matter of fact ——

Mapp What?

Georgie Well, it's not settled or anything. Perhaps I oughtn't to talk about it yet.

Mapp Mr Pillson, I'm the soul of discretion.

Georgie Yes, but I don't really believe in *talking* about things till they've *happened*.

Mapp (*coyly*) Shall I make a guess?

Georgie Why — did you see me looking at it?

Mapp *It*, Mr Pillson? What's it?

Georgie The — why, what did *you* mean?

Mapp I've seen you looking at *her*.

Georgie Her? Who? I mean, *whom*?

Mapp Oh, Mr Pillson, that's not fair. You know who — I mean, *whom*.

Georgie No, I swear I don't. Do you mean Lucia? Oh, you don't think — you can't mean —— ?

Mapp Am I wrong?

Georgie Oh, but completely. I assure you. Such an idea has never occurred to either of us.

Mapp To *either* of you?

Georgie No — why? You don't think *she* ... ? (*Alarmed*) Oh, my goodness, she hasn't *said* anything to you, has she?

Mapp Not a word.

Georgie Then what on earth made you think —— ?

Mapp (*rising*) Mr Pillson, forgive me. I see I was wrong. Completely wrong. I'm sorry I said anything. But what were *you* talking about? That you said wasn't settled?

Georgie Oh, that. Well, it's just an idea. I was looking at that little white cottage next door. I see it's to be let furnished, and I thought ——

Mapp You thought you might take it. To be near Lucia—I mean, Mrs Lucas.

Georgie Yes, but not in that way. Really not. I *must* ask you to get any such ideas out of your head. Our friendship's nothing like that.

Mapp (*coyly*) Is there someone else somewhere?

Georgie No, no, really. On my word, there isn't.

Mapp You mean, we may have a completely unattached bachelor in our midst? (*She sits on the sofa*) Oh, Mr Pillson, you don't know what that will do to the ladies of Tilling.

Georgie (*very pleased with this*) Oh, really! (*He giggles*)

The door is heard closing off UL

Mapp (*rising*) Oh, there's the front door.

Georgie That will be Lucia. (*He goes to the arch; calling off* L) Lucia?

Lucia (*off* UL) Si, Georgino mio. Io son.

Lucia enters through the arch from L. *She carries a parasol and full shopping basket*

Caro, come sta? (*Seeing Mapp*) Oh, Miss Mapp.

Mapp Good-morning, dear Mrs Lucas. I just popped in to see how you were getting along. Mr Pillson has been entertaining me. And you, I see, have been the busy little bee, exploring our quaint little shopping street.

Lucia It's all too fascinating. I bought a shopping basket. I had to. (*She puts the basket on the desk*) Georgie, the Tilling ladies all do their shopping themselves, instead of having the tradesmen call for orders.

Mapp Oh, we wouldn't miss our morning shopping. That's when we do all our gossiping.

Georgie So I noticed. Little knots on every corner, talking away.

Lucia I longed to join them. Poor little newcomer me felt quite left out in the cold.

Mapp I'm sure that won't be for long. (*Crossing to Lucia*) Only, dear Mrs Lucas, if I might offer a word of warning …

Lucia Yes?

Mapp Well, the other residents here … Of course, they're all my dearest friends, and I'm absolutely devoted to them … but it's just possible that they may try to "rush" you a little. If you would care for me to take you under my wing, tell you who's who … So tiresome in a new place if one makes mistakes, don't you think?

Lucia (*whose eyes have grown slightly glacial during this*) I'm afraid I don't really know. I'm not in the habit of making mistakes about people.

Georgie, scenting the snub, coughs and moves up to the arch

Mapp (*rebuffed, but trying not to show it*) Oh, I'm quite sure of that. I only meant ——

Lucia Quite. And it was very kind of you. (*Moving to the sofa*) But in any case, I am not proposing to lead an extensive social life here. (*She notices the reversed sofa cushions and turns them back again from the yellow to the brown side*) Peace and quiet are all I ask. To study my beloved Dante, and my divine Beethoven … (*going to the french windows*) … and to wander in my *giardino*. Oh, that means my garden. *Your* giardino, really. Your charming giardino.

Mapp Yes, it is generally conceded to be rather the pride of the town, though I do say it myself.

Lucia (*pointing to the easel with her parasol*) I was trying to capture it this morning on canvas. (*She sits on the sofa and puts the parasol down*) Well, caro, did you try that sketch I suggested of the quaint house with the crooked chimney?

Georgie (*moving to Lucia*) Yes, I've done it, Lucia. But I'm not sure I shouldn't have made the chimney straight. Otherwise, people might think it was an accident.

Mapp The crooked chimney! It's quite a favourite subject with us all. We all paint here, you know. I didn't know you were an artist, too, Mr Pillson.

Georgie Oh, my dear, I just fiddle. Lucia's the one who wins all the prizes.

Mapp Indeed? Well, then, you must both promise to let me have something for our Art Exhibition. It's the big event of the year here. All local talent, you know, and I'm the *President*.

Lucia I'm sure we'd be delighted.

Mapp You know, Mr Pillson, I was thinking. That little plan you told me of just now. You haven't been to the house-agent's yet, have you?

Georgie No, I was going this afternoon.

Mapp Well, I was wondering — Isabel Poppit, the owner, is quite a friend of mine. If you would prefer to deal with her direct, I'm sure we could get it quite cheap. Suppose I ring her up and see if she's at home? Then we could pop round straight away. Will you excuse me?

Lucia Of course.

Mapp exits UR

What's *she* doing here? (*She removes her hat and gloves during the following and puts them on the sofa*)

Georgie I don't know. I found her here.

Lucia Yes, she's been in and out of this house three times a day ever since I moved in. Taking little things she forgot — wanting to see what things of hers I've put away. Believe me, I haven't begun! The rubbish that there is! And, Georgie, her taste in books!

Georgie (*sitting on the sofa*) Yes, so I noticed. Not one decent binding! And the only *poetry* in the house seems to be Kipling's *Barrack Room Ballads*. So vulgar.

Lucia She seems to have a *passion* for Kipling. There's a framed copy of "If" in the — upstairs place to wash your hands.

Georgie My dear, how very disconcerting.

Lucia But nothing like as disconcerting as these "poppings" in and out of here. And the way she seems to want to "take me over". No, that won't do. That won't do at all. Why did you tell her about taking the cottage?

Georgie I don't know. It came up.

Lucia How?

Georgie Well, she was talking about — about my ... (*He rises, embarrassed*) I don't remember.

Lucia Have you really decided to take the cottage?

Georgie Well, if I were quite sure that Foljambe wouldn't mind. She's such a perfect parlour-maid, I'd hate to do anything to upset her.

Lucia Georgie, surely you must have noticed that Foljambe and Cadman are sweet on each other? (*She rises and goes to Georgie*) Well, as Cadman will be here as my chauffeur, I can't think of anything that would make Foljambe happier.

Georgie Oh, well, that's wonderful, then.

Lucia Wonderful for me, too, Georgie. To have you right next door.

Georgie looks frightened

Why do you look like that?

Georgie Like what?

Lucia I don't know. But you looked almost — frightened, for a minute.

Mapp enters UR

Georgie and Lucia break L *a few steps*

Mapp Everything's settled. Sweet Isabel is expecting us. Will you forgive me, dear Mrs Lucas, if I carry Mr Pillson off? I won't keep him long.

Lucia Of course. Ring for Grosvenor, will you, Georgie?

Georgie starts for the bell by the fireplace, but Mapp stops him

Mapp Please don't bother. Such formality between friends. We are friends, I hope?

Lucia (*smiling, but with implication*) I hope so.

Mapp Well, then, I'll say "au reservoir".

Lucia What?

Mapp I just said "au reservoir". A little local joke. We all say it.

Lucia Oh, I see.

Mapp (*looking out the window* L) Oh, dear, here's Major Benjy back again.

Lucia *Back* again?

Mapp He was here earlier. I told him it was no hour for a call. You mustn't let him pester you, dear Mrs Lucas.

Lucia I thought the major very charming.

Georgie (*disapproving*) Oh, did you, Lucia?

Mapp (*to Georgie*) Up to now he's been our only bachelor, and he's been rather spoiled, you know. (*To Lucia*) As a matter of fact, there's a silly idea ——

Lucia What?

Mapp (*still to Lucia*) It's all nonsense, of course. You know what a small town like this is like. But, well, as I say, there *is* an idea that he's supposed to be smitten with *me*. Too silly. (*Quickly, to Georgie*) Ready, Mr Georgie? (*She goes towards the arch*)

Georgie Quite. (*To Lucia, moving to the arch*) Well, a riverderla.

Lucia A riverderci, Georgino mio.

Mapp How lovely to be able to talk Italian like that! Come along, Mr Georgie.

Mapp takes Georgie's arm and hustles him off through the arch to L

Georgie (*off* UL *to Major*) Good-morning.

Major (*off* UL *to Georgie*) Good-morning.

Mapp (*off* UL) Back again already, Major?

Major (*off* UL *to Mapp*) Yes. Mrs Lucas at home?

Lucia (*on the lower step, looking into the hall*) Good-morning, Major. Come in, won't you?

Major (*off* UL) Thanks.

The Major enters through the arch from L. *He carries his "Diaries" manuscript*

Lucia (*extending her hand*) How do you do.

Major (*shaking hands*) How do you do.

Lucia (*moving to the love-seat*) You wanted to see me?

Major (*following*) Just wanted to bring you these old diaries I was talking about. (*He hands the manuscript to her*)

Lucia (*sitting on the love-seat and opening the manuscript*) How delightful. I shall look forward to reading them.

Major All right if I stay for a minute?

Lucia Of course. Pull up a chair, will you?

Major (*fetching the desk chair and placing it with the back of chair to the audience*) Well, how are you shaking down here, Mrs Lucas? What do you think of our little town of Tilling?

Lucia (*closing the manuscript and putting it on the love-seat*) I think it's charming. Of course, I've seen very little of it yet …

Major Won't take you long to get the hang of it. (*He straddles the chair, facing front*) Place is really run by a sort of select few, if you know what I mean. Mr and Mrs Wyse — the old couple who were here yesterday — they're the sort of leaders here. Money, you know. Simply rolling in it. Then there's the vicar and his wife. They're the people to get in with, if you're really planning to take us over.

Lucia Take you over?

Major That's what Mapp's been saying. You're supposed to run the whole show in the place you live, and as *she*'s always tried to run the whole show here, she's a bit alarmed at the idea that you're going to depose her, don't you know.

Lucia But what absolute nonsense. Perhaps, in Riseholme, they did rather insist on my taking the lead in their little activities. But *here* — oh, no. Miss Mapp can rely on my taking a very humble back seat.

Major That's a bit of a pity, if you ask me. (*He rises*) Liz is a fine woman, but — well, don't say I said so, but a bit of new blood might be a godsend here. Of course, you *have* been a godsend in one way already.

Lucia *I* have?

Major Coming and taking this house. We all let our houses here in the summer, you know, and move around. Sort of like musical chairs, don't you know. So, when you took Mapp's house, she took old Diva Plaistow's, and Diva took mine, and I moved into one opposite, and — well, as we all get more rent than we pay, you're something of a public benefactor.

Lucia How quaint.

Major (*looking at his watch*) Well, I'd better be toddling along.

Lucia (*rising and ringing the bell by the fireplace*) Thank you for all the information, Major. It's been most instructive.

Major You'll keep it to yourself, won't you? Wouldn't want anyone to think I'd been gossiping. One thing I can't stand is gossip. Get too much of it round here as it is.

Lucia I quite understand, Major.

Major Mind if I go out through the garden? I'm having lunch with old Isabel Poppit — that white cottage next door. She's the only one who hasn't let yet. You don't know anyone who'd like to take it, do you? It's only four guineas a week.

Lucia I might know someone.

Major I'll look in again, if I may. I hope to see a lot more of you, Mrs Lucas.

Lucia Thank you, Major. I hope so, too.

Major That will be tophole. Well, toodle-oo.

He exits through the french window

Lucia replaces the chair at the desk

Grosvenor enters UR

Grosvenor You rang, madam?

Lucia Oh, yes, Grosvenor. You might take my hat and gloves — and my shopping basket. (*She picks up the basket from the desk*)

Grosvenor Very good, madam. (*She picks up Lucia's hat, gloves and parasol from the sofa*)

Lucia By the way, Grosvenor, when Miss Mapp called this morning, did she ring or just walk in?

Grosvenor (*taking the basket from Lucia*) I think she must have walked in, madam. I found her in here. She was looking at your letters.

Lucia My letters? (*She goes to the desk and picks up the mail*)

Grosvenor She asked me a lot of questions, madam. About you and whether ...

Lucia Whether what?

Grosvenor Well, madam, about whether you were thinking of marrying again.

Lucia (*putting the mail back on the desk*) What?

Grosvenor Well, madam, I think she thinks you and Mr Pillson may be getting married.

Lucia Mr ... ? Did she say that?

Grosvenor Not in so many words, madam. But she seemed to be hinting at it.

Lucia I see. Thank you, Grosvenor.

Grosvenor Very good, madam.

Grosvenor exits through the arch to R

Lucia (*to herself*) Georgie! Oh, it's absurd!

Georgie starts to enter through the french window

Surely *he* can't want —— (*She turns and sees Georgie*) Oh, Georgie! Well, what happened?

Georgie (*sitting in the armchair* DR *and putting his hat on the side-table*) It's all settled. I've taken it. It's quite sweet, it really is. Little rooms, all up and down. Quite pictureskew.

Lucia Splendid!

Georgie And not really expensive. Only six guineas.

Lucia How much?

Georgie Six guineas.

Lucia Are you sure?

Georgie Of course I'm sure. Why?

Lucia (*sitting on the sofa*) Oh, Georgie, there's Miss Mapp again! The woman was asking four.

Georgie How do you know?

Lucia The gossiping Major just told me. Of course! That's what Mapp telephoned about. That's why she said not to go to the house-agent.

Georgie I don't believe it.

Lucia Ring up the agent and ask.

Georgie I will. (*He rises and starts* UR *then stops*) No, I won't. If it's true, it'll only upset me. There's nothing I can do about it now. I've said I'd take it. If I've been cheated, I'd rather not know.

Lucia (*amused*) Well, that's a point of view.

Georgie But what a serpent! Do you suppose they're splitting the difference between them?

Lucia Yes, I do.

Georgie And I thought I was getting such a bargain. I even offered her a commission.

Lucia You don't mean to say she didn't take it?

Georgie She said she'd like my painting of the crooked chimney. She said that was all she'd accept. Oh, but she's a horrible woman, Lucia! You talk about her trying to take *you* over. You should have seen the way she treated *me*. I might have been her property.

Lucia By the way, Georgie, was anything said between you about *us*? You and me, I mean?

Georgie (*nervously*) *What* about us?

Lucia Oh, anything. Our — friendship, or anything.

Georgie (*vaguely*) Oh, she talked a lot of nonsense, but ——

Lucia (*firmly, but in baby-talk*) Georgie, I tink you and I have got to have an ickle chat.

Georgie Oh, dear. *Must* we?

Lucia I tink so.

She beckons to him. He moves to the sofa

Georgie, you and I have been friends for more years than perhaps either of us would care to admit to. I want you to know that I'm very grateful for that friendship.

Georgie (*formally*) I am, too. It's been extremely pleasant.

Lucia You're rather alone in the world, and so am I.

Georgie looks alarmed

But we're both rather set in our ways. I don't think we'd want to change them.

A gleam of hope comes to Georgie

It seems to me that our friendship is perfect just as it is.

Georgie (*with relief*) Oh, I do so agree with you!

Lucia Not that I think you ever had any other idea, really. But — well, being a widow, and not wholly unattractive, does make a difference, I suppose. And I wouldn't want you to think that I had been — well, leading you on. That's why I *had* to say this.

Georgie (*with great relief, sitting next to Lucia on the sofa*) My dear, it's exactly what I wanted to hear. I've *never* thought that you were leading me on, but after what *she* said this morning, I did wonder whether perhaps *you* thought that *I* — well, I mean ... (*He breaks off, embarrassed*)

Lucia Georgie, we don't need to say any more. We understand each other perfectly, just as I always thought we did.

Georgie Lucia, I think you're marvellous! (*He kisses her hand*) I'm so glad now that I've taken the cottage. I don't care if I have been cheated. But you will protect me from Miss Mapp, won't you?

Lucia Yes, Georgie, I'll protect you. I'll take care of Miss Mapp in *every* way. You know, I think I'm going to have rather a good time here, one way and another. (*She looks at her watch*) And now we've still half an hour before lunch. Let's have some musica. (*She rises and goes to the piano*)

Georgie Musica! (*He rises and goes to the piano*)

Lucia We've been neglecting it quite dreadfully. Suppose we try this one. (*She hands him the "Beethoven" music book from the piano*)

Georgie (*putting on his glasses and scanning the music*) What is it?

Lucia (*putting on her glasses from the piano*) Divine Beethoven. But you'll have to be patient with me. It's so long since I looked at it.

Georgie So long? But this is the one I heard you practising last night.

Lucia (*back in baby talk*) Needs practice. Lucia's part dweffy diffy.

Georgie Georgie's part diffy, too. Bass much more diffy than treble. (*He removes his rings and puts them on the piano*) Full of nasty, horrid accidentals.

Both sit on the piano bench and place their hands on the keyboard

Lucia Are you ready?

Georgie Yes. (*He giggles*)

Lucia Now then — Uno — due — tre!

They start to play a duet (the Second Movement, from Beethoven's "Symphony No. 8"). After a few bars ——

— the CURTAIN *falls*

SCENE 2

DEPUTATION SCENE

The same. Morning. Four weeks later

As the CURTAIN *rises, Mr Wyse is standing* R *of the sofa, Lucia is seated on the* R *end of sofa, Mrs Wyse is seated on the* L *end of the sofa, the Vicar and Evie are seated on the love-seat*

Mr Wyse So you see us, dear Mrs Lucas, as it were, upon our bended knees. The hospital is sorely in need of money. A garden party would be the ideal thing.

Lucia Yes, I see, Mr Wyse, but why come to *me*? I am only a newcomer here.

Mr Wyse Speaking by the calendar, that may be true. But in the all too short time you have been with us, you have proved yourself a veritable Aspasia.

Mrs Wyse Yes, indeed!

Mr Wyse The festivities with which you have regaled us — dinners, musicales, bridge parties ——

Mrs Wyse Tilling has never known anything like it!

Vicar (*in Scots dialect*) Ay, Tilling's a new toon, that it is!

Lucia I beg your pardon?

Evie He means it's a new town!

Vicar (*rising*) That's what I mean! I forgot, Mrs Lucas, you're not used to my sense of humour yet.

Evie Talking in Scotch is his sense of humour!

Mr Wyse We have long needed a leading spirit here.

Lucia You're all being very kind. But I should have thought almost anyone — for instance, Miss Mapp ——

Evie giggles

Mr Wyse (*evasively*) Miss Mapp is a most energetic lady — but the question is, may we look to you?

Lucia Naturally, my services are completely at your disposal for the hospital.

Mr Wyse Capital!

Lucia (*pointing towards the garden*) *This* garden, for instance. Would that be a suitable place, do you think?

Mr Wyse The ideal spot! But unfortunately its use for such a purpose has never been permitted. (*To Mrs Wyse*) Am I right, my dear?

Mrs Wyse Quite right.

Evie Miss Mapp's never allowed it. (*She giggles*)

Lucia (*after a tiny pause*) And the entertainment. I produced some tableaux last year at Riseholme that people were kind enough to praise. I'm sure Mr Pillson and I would be only too glad to repeat some of them.

Mr Wyse (*sitting in the armchair*) I was trying to summon up courage to suggest exactly that!

Lucia And, let me see — what else?

Evie Kenneth could tell some Scotch stories.

Lucia Would you, Vicar?

Vicar Hoots, toots, ye'll no be wanting to hear ma old chestnuts.

Mrs Wyse Oh, but we will, Vicar. I can never hear them too often.

Vicar Well, perhaps to fill in between the tableaux, while ye're changing your clothes.

Lucia Splendid!

Evie He does Scotch *songs*, too. Harry Lauder.

Vicar Hold yer whisht, wee wifie.

Evie He does!

Lucia Well, then, we must have those, too.

Evie And he imitates the bagpipes.

Lucia Well — !

Mrs Wyse Oh, and Diva Plaistow. Her imitation of the seasick lady with an orange. I always laugh when I see that.

Lucia Well, I think we shall have more than enough, anyway.

Mr Wyse (*rising*) And now, Susan, we must not trespass any longer upon Mrs Lucas' valuable time.

Simultaneously: Lucia rises, and rings the bell; Evie rises and moves to the Vicar; Mrs Wyse rises

Mrs Wyse No, indeed. (*She goes to the arch*)

Vicar I'll start the choir rehearsing glees and madrigals this verra afternoon.

Mr Wyse (*shaking hands with Lucia*) Mille grazie, dear lady! Mille grazie! You see what else you have done to us? You'll have us all chattering away in Italian like yourself in no time.

Grosvenor enters through the arch from R

Lucia Oh, Grosvenor, will you show Mr and Mrs Wyse and Mr and Mrs Bartlett out, please?

Grosvenor Very good, madam. (*She starts to go*)
Lucia And, Grosvenor!

Grosvenor stops

   Don't forget to put the chain back on the door.
Grosvenor Very good, madam.

   Grosvenor exits through the arch to L, *followed by Mr Wyse and Mrs Wyse*

Vicar Ye're a grand woman, Mistress Lucas, and Tilling will sing your
   praises till the Day of Judgment. (*To Evie*) Come awa', wee wifie.

   The Vicar exits through the arch to L

Evie (*shaking hands with Lucia*) Goodbye. It's so wonderful! I don't know
   what Miss Mapp's going to say!

   Evie giggles and exits through the arch to L

Lucia (*stretching and basking, to herself*) How they all work me! (*She moves
   towards the desk*)

   Georgie enters through the french window

Georgie Is the coast clear? May I come in?
Lucia Oh, Georgie, of course.
Georgie (*removing his hat, sitting on the sofa*) I saw them all go. What was
   that about? They looked like a deputation.
Lucia They were. The most important people in the town.

   Georgie sighs and puts his feet up on the sofa

   But what's the matter? You look upset about something.
Georgie I am. It's Foljambe. She's being so tarsome. She's suddenly decided
   she doesn't like it here, and wants to go back to Riseholme. And if *she* goes,
   I'll have to go, too.
Lucia Oh, Georgie, you can't be so dependent on your parlour-maid.
Georgie (*moving his feet off the sofa, sitting up*) I've a very dependent nature.
   I couldn't live without her. She cried dreadfully this morning when she
   brought me my tea. The bread and butter was absolutely sopping.
Lucia (*over his left shoulder*) She's probably had a tiff with Cadman. We'll
   give them the same night off, and let him take her out in the car. That'll do
   it, you see.

Georgie Oh, I do hope so. (*He kisses her hand*) Lucia, you are a comfort.

Lucia goes to the love-seat. Georgie throws his hat on to the piano

By the way, what's the idea of putting the chain on the front door? I came round that way first.

Lucia (*sitting on the love-seat*) That's something else. But what made you come round the front? You never do.

Georgie No. I just thought it might look better. (*He rises and sits on the arm of the sofa*) After all, Lucia, using the garden door and coming in here through the window — well, it does look a little *clandestino*.

Lucia What utter nonsense! Who knows you come across the garden, anyway?

Georgie (*rising*) Everyone, it seems.

Lucia Who told them?

Georgie Mapp.

Lucia I thought so. How does *she* know?

Georgie I've no idea, unless she stands on her roof with opera-glasses. But she's been gossiping like mad. It's all because I've refused to be alone with her. Never seen her without your being there. This is her revenge. Hell holds no fury like a woman scorned.

Lucia But *I* haven't scorned her. I don't see why she should traduce *me*.

Georgie Oh, my dear, she loathes you — because of the success you've made here.

Lucia (*naïvely*) Success? I?

Georgie Oh, come off it, Lucia. For someone who wanted only peace and quiet, you've done more entertaining and been more entertained than ten duchesses. And she's absolutely livid.

Lucia (*rising*) I'm afraid she's going to get a little livider. I'm going to have to give Miss Elizabeth Mapp a few sharp slaps.

Georgie (*kneeling on the love-seat*) Why, what's been happening? Tell me. I'm all agog!

Lucia In the first place, I think I've caught her cheating me over the rent.

Georgie What — you, too?

Lucia Rents here are supposed to include garden produce, I've discovered. And then there's the way she gushes all over me. She calls me "Lulu" now, and that I really will not stand. I'm going to start calling her "Liblib", and see if that will stop her.

Georgie Oo, lovely! Liblib! (*He giggles*)

Lucia And, lastly, the "popping" habit has started again.

Georgie Popping? In *here*, you mean?

Lucia Yes. She's got a new excuse now. Wanting things for that absurd Jumble Sale of hers.

Georgie Oh, yes, that starts today, doesn't it?

Lucia And she never rings the bell, either. Just pops in. That's why I put the chain on the door. Now she won't be able to *get* in without ringing.

The sound of the door being forced open and the crash of a broken chain is heard off UL. *Georgie rises*

What on earth's that?

Mapp falls into the room through arch from L *and staggers to the love-seat, where Georgie catches her*

Elizabeth, what *are* you doing?

Georgie releases her

Mapp (*to Georgie*) Thank you. (*To Lucia*) Lulu, dear, I must apologize. So humbly. Such a stupid accident. I tried to open your front door, and gave it just a teeny little push, and your servants must have forgotten to take the chain down. I'm afraid I broke something. The chain must have been rusty. (*To Georgie*) Good-morning, Mr Georgie.

Georgie Good-morning.

Lucia But I don't understand. Didn't Grosvenor come to open the door when you rang?

Mapp I'm afraid that's just what I forgot to do, dear. You and I are such friends, and so hard always to remember that it's not my own house, any more.

Lucia Let me see what damage you've done.

Lucia exits through the arch to L

Mapp You're quite the early bird, aren't you, Mr Georgie? Did you and Lulu have breakfast together?

Georgie I always have *my* breakfast in bed.

Mapp Yes, so I've heard. Lulu does, too, doesn't she?

Lucia enters through the arch from L. *She carries a section of the door chain*

Lucia No sign of rust at all. I shall have to send for the ironmonger, and get him to make the chain stronger.

Mapp You must let me pay for it.

Lucia (*coldly*) Naturally. (*She puts the chain on the sofa side-table*) Now, Elizabeth, what did you want to see me about?

Mapp I didn't want to see you at all, dear. I just wanted to run upstairs and get some little thing for my Jumble Sale. Such a success it's being. But no need to bother *you*.

Lucia (*firmly*) Elizabeth, I'm sorry, but I really cannot have any more of these "little trips upstairs". I agreed that you should lock up your private belongings, but not that you should come and *un*lock them every five minutes.

Mapp Lulu, surely we don't need to go into our little domestic details in front of Mr Georgie.

Lucia Oh, I've no secrets from Georgie.

Georgie Perhaps I'd better ... (*He makes a move to go*)

Lucia No, Georgie, you stay here. I'm not in the habit of asking my friends to leave.

Georgie sits on the pouffe. Lucia sits on the sofa

Now, Elizabeth, let us come to an understanding. You know I'm always delighted to see you, but I cannot have you, or anyone else, popping in here uninvited at all hours of the day and night.

Mapp (*with a glance at Georgie*) Unless they use the *garden* door, I suppose?

Georgie rises

Lucia If that's one of your little jokes, Elizabeth, I don't think it's very funny.

Mapp (*after a moment*) Very well, ruthless one. It shall be as you wish. Exactly as you wish. No argument. No argument at all.

Lucia Good. And if you really want things for your Jumble Sale, why go upstairs? The whole house is full of stuff that I should think would do beautifully.

Mapp Thank you, dear. But, as a matter of fact, (*with another glance at Georgie*) I've just thought of something I have at home that will do perfectly. Well ——

Lucia rises. Mapp goes to Lucia and shakes hands

—— au reservoir, dear Lulu.

Lucia Goodbye, Liblib.

Mapp (*breaking the handshake abruptly*) What an extraordinary name. No-one has ever called me that before.

Lucia No-one has ever called me "Lulu" before.

Mapp Oh, perhaps you'd rather I called you Emmeline? That *is* your name, I believe. (*Moving up to the arch*) Well, au reservoir, Mr Georgie. Perhaps you'll come and dine with me some night, if dear Emmeline will allow you? You can come in by the front door. There will be no chain up.

Mapp exits through the arch to L

Georgie That was a nasty one.

Lucia (*sitting on the sofa*) She's a nasty woman, I'm afraid, Georgie. How did you think I managed her?

Georgie (*sitting on the love-seat*) Beautifully. So sweet and dignified. I was lost in admiration of you. I hope she won't take it out on *me*, though. If she goes on spreading scandal ... She said something, while you were out of the room, about breakfast in bed, that quite made me blush.

Lucia Georgie, you blush too easily. (*She rises and picks up Georgie's hat from the piano*) Now why don't you nip over to her Jumble Sale, and see if there isn't something you can pick up?

Georgie rises and moves to Lucia

And be very, very sweet to dear Liblib. You can afford to be, having just seen her worsted like that. Poor Liblib.

Georgie (*taking his hat from Lucia*) She hated that, didn't she? Though it was rather sharp of her to think of calling you Emmeline.

Lucia That, Georgie, was hitting below the belt.

Diva is heard off UL

Diva (*off* UL) Lucia, are you at home? It's me, Diva Plaistow, and Major Benjy. Can we come in?

Lucia Of course, come in.

Georgie Major Benjy! (*He moves up to* R *of the arch*)

Diva enters through the arch from L. *She carries a string shopping bag and a half-eaten chocolate biscuit*

Diva Good-morning, Lucia. Good-morning, Mr Georgie.

Georgie Good-morning. (*He puts on his hat*) Just off to the Jumble Sale.

Georgie exits through the arch to L. *He is heard talking to the Major in the hall*

(*Off*) Good-morning.

Major (*off* UL *to Georgie*) Good-morning.

The Major enters through the arch from L

Diva We're not disturbing you, are we?

Lucia No, of course not. Good-morning, Major.

Major Good-morning.

Lucia What brings you both here?

Diva Just been having coffee and chocky bickies at the Tea Shoppe opposite. Saw Elizabeth come storming out of here, looking like a dose of castor oil. (*She sits on the love-seat*) Had to find out what it was all about. (*She eats the biscuit*)

Lucia (*amused*) You, too, Major?

Major Well, couldn't help being curious, you know. Wondered what was going on, and all that.

Lucia It was just a little accident. It so happened that I had a chain on the front door this morning, and dear Elizabeth gave herself rather a nasty jolt against it. I'm afraid she may have hurt herself.

Major (*pushing the pouffe to the love-seat*) Oh, I say, that's too bad.

Lucia I must send her something. (*She sits on the sofa*) What are her favourite flowers, Major?

Major (*sitting on the pouffe*) Well, I don't know about flowers, but she's very keen on strawberries. Garden here's full of strawberry beds. You might send her some of those.

Lucia But she gets those already. The gardener picks them for her every morning.

Diva What do you mean? Doesn't she *give* you garden produce?

Lucia No, just flowers for the house. That's all.

Diva Well, really! She distinctly told me — no, she didn't, I'll be fair to her. I asked her if she was giving you garden produce, because she's getting it from me, and she said naturally she wasn't going to dig up all her potatoes. Of course, I thought that meant she *was* giving it to you.

Lucia Well, what do a few silly pears and strawberries matter, anyway?

Diva It isn't the pears, it's the principle! Gets my house with garden produce thrown in for eight guineas, and lets hers to you without produce for ten.

Lucia No, I pay twelve.

Major (*rising*) *What's that?*

Diva There! That's what I mean. She distinctly told me — no, she didn't, I remember. I asked her what she was getting from you, and she said you had closed with the figure she asked.

Lucia So I did. She asked twelve. But aren't we making rather too much of this?

Diva Not a bit. If she gets more than ten from you, she ought to pay me more than eight.

Major And Diva ought to pay me more than six.

Lucia (*to the Major*) And *you* ought to pay whoever's house you've taken more than you are paying them. So it seems to me that *they're* the only ones who are really suffering.

Major Except *you*.

Lucia Well, I'm not complaining. (*She rises*) I think if dear Elizabeth has been clever enough to get a few extra guineas for herself, we shouldn't grudge them to her.

Major By Jove, Mrs Lucas, I think you're wonderful, taking it like that. If the boot were on the other foot, I bet she'd be ready to scratch your eyes out.

Lucia Oh, no, Major, I'm sure she wouldn't.

Major Well, she's not the saint you are, Mrs Lucas. Not by a long shot.

Diva rises

Well, I'll say "Addio, donna bellissima". How's that for an old soldier man?

Lucia It's wonderful, Major!

The Major goes to the arch

Diva Well, au reservoir. (*Moving to the arch*) Can't wait to tell everyone what you've told us.

Diva exits through the arch to L

Lucia goes to the Major. They shake hands

Major Goodbye.

Diva (*off* UL) Hallo, Mr Georgie. Didn't take you long.

Georgie (*off* UL) No.

Georgie enters through the arch from L. *His hat is on, and he carries a hearth-brush, several curtain rings on a string, and his "Crooked Chimney" picture*

Major Back already?

Georgie You still here?

The Major exits through the arch to L

Lucia, I've got something to show you!

Lucia What on earth have you got there?

Georgie Things from Elizabeth's Jumble Sale. You never saw such rubbish. But I thought I ought to buy *something*, so I went to the sixpenny tray and bought a hearth-brush — (*he puts the hearth-brush on the desk*) and some curtain rings — (*he puts the curtain rings on the desk*) And then what do you think I found?

Lucia What?

Georgie (*holding up the picture*) My crooked chimney! That I gave her as a reward for doing me out of two guineas a week rent. For sixpence. Sixpence! Why, the frame cost a shilling! (*He takes out his handkerchief and dusts the picture*)

Lucia (*sitting on the love-seat*) How perfectly monstrous!

Georgie *This* must be what she thought of just now to put in the Jumble Sale. She did it out of spite. She must have rushed straight home from here, snatched it off the wall, and thrown it into the sixpenny tray!

Lucia It's the pettiest thing I ever heard of, in all my life!

Georgie Well, I know one thing — (*He touches his head and realizes he still has hat on*) Oh, I *beg* your pardon! (*He removes his hat and places it on the desk*) Well, I know one thing. I won't send anything to the Art Exhibition now. She's the President. And I hope you won't send anything, either. Let them find their own beastly pictures!

Lucia No, Georgie. The Art Exhibition is the big event of the year. We can't afford to be left out of it. In fact, I think you should submit that very same picture.

Georgie Why? She'll only turn it down.

Lucia I don't think she'll be able to.

Georgie Why won't she?

Lucia She may be the President, but Mr and Mrs Wyse are on the Hanging Committee with her, and they *need* you and me at the moment for a garden party. So they're absolutely bound to vote for your picture — *and* mine — and that will be the best way of snubbing Elizabeth. (*She rises*) You know, I don't think people here would mind seeing her taken down a peg or two. I've started a little story on its rounds this morning that won't do her any good. (*She sits on the sofa*) I've got all the leading spirits of the town on my side. And, I've even got her special friend, the Major, thinking that I'm wonderful. So I think dear Elizabeth had better start looking to her laurels.

Georgie Lucia, you're having too much fun!

Lucia What do you mean? You know I don't *enjoy* this sort of thing.

Georgie smiles

And don't look at me like that, Georgie. I don't like it. Why don't you ring for some sherry? You're staying to lunch, aren't you?

Georgie No, I told Foljambe I'd be home to lunch.

Lucia I'm all alone.

Georgie I don't think I'd better upset her plans today. Besides, she's got sweetbreads for me.

The bell sounds off UL

Lucia Was that the bell?

Georgie (*looking out the window* L) It's the Major again. *He* seems to have caught the popping habit now. (*He puts the picture on the desk*) What did you mean — he thinks you're wonderful?

Grosvenor crosses through the arch from R *to* L

Lucia He said so. Ridiculous of him, I know, but ... you don't mind, do you?

Georgie (*weakly*) No, but ——

The Major is heard off UL

Major (*off* UL) Is Mrs Lucas at home?

Grosvenor (*off* UL) Yes, sir. Will you come in?

Grosvenor enters through the arch from L

Major Flint, madam.

Lucia Bring in some sherry, will you Grosvenor?

Grosvenor Very good, madam.

Grosvenor exits UR

The Major enters through the arch from L, *carrying a box of strawberries*

Major Back again like the bad penny, Mrs Lucas. But I just thought I'd bring you this box of strawberries. (*To Georgie*) Oh, hallo.

Georgie (*coldly*) How do you do.

Lucia (*taking the box of strawberries*) How very kind of you, Major. (*She peeps at them*) These look beautiful. Why don't you stay to lunch and we can have them then?

Major (*with a look at Georgie*) Well, I ——

Lucia I'm all by myself.

Major Oh, well, in that case, I'd like to. Thanks.

Georgie starts collecting the hat, picture, hearth-brush, and curtain rings from the desk

Lucia Splendid! (*Indicating the love-seat*) Sit down, won't you?

The Major sits on the love-seat

It's very nice of you to take pity on me.

Major Shouldn't have thought *you'd* ever want for company, Mrs Lucas.

Having collected the items from the desk, Georgie moves away

Masculine company, anyway.

Georgie freezes at c

Grosvenor enters UR *with a tray holding a decanter of sherry and three glasses. She puts the tray on the side table*

Lucia Thank you, Grosvenor. And will you take this box of strawberries? (*She hands the box to Grosvenor*) We'll have them for lunch. Major Flint is staying.

Grosvenor Very good, madam. Will Mr Pillson be staying, too?

Lucia No, Grosvenor.

Georgie (*suddenly*) Yes! Yes, I think I *will* stay, after all! (*He gives the Major a look and deposits his armful of things on the piano*)

Lucia Oh? Three for lunch, then, Grosvenor.

Grosvenor Very good, madam.

Grosvenor exits UR

Lucia How nice, Georgie. But what about Foljambe?

Georgie Oh, she can eat her own sweetbreads. (*He goes to the sherry on side-table*) Besides, I like strawberries better.

Major (*sulkily*) Don't know that there'll be enough for *three*.

Lucia I'm sure we can make them go round.

Georgie pours two glasses of sherry

Major (*rising*) You know, Mrs Lucas, I'm afraid you're in for a spot of trouble.

Lucia Oh?

Major Seems you're going to have a garden-party here. Just heard about it, in the greengrocer's. Liz was there, too. And — well, I'm afraid she's not too pleased about it. Always refused to lend her garden for anything like that.

Georgie picks up two glasses of sherry and gives one to Lucia

Lucia Oh, I'd no idea.
Major Expressed herself pretty strongly about it, just now. (*He sits on the love-seat*) I'm rather afraid this means *war*, Mrs Lucas.
Georgie (*handing the other sherry glass to the Major*) I think the war has started already.
Lucia War? What nonsense!
Major You don't know Liz when she gets her back up.
Georgie (*laughing*) And you don't know Lucia when she ——
Lucia (*interrupting, sharply*) When she *what*, Georgie?
Georgie (*to the Major*) I just meant — you don't know Lucia. (*He pours himself a glass of sherry*)
Major No, but I hope to, what? (*He bursts forth with a loud laugh*)

Georgie, picking up his glass of sherry, turns and glares at the Major, who freezes and then rises

Well, let's have a toast, what? Not taking sides or anything, but suppose we say — may the best woman win?

The Major and Georgie start to raise their glasses

Lucia (*to the Major, taking this to herself; smiling delightedly*) Oh, *thank* you. (*Then to Georgie*) Thank you!

The Major and Georgie raise their glasses and sip

CURTAIN

ACT II
Scene 1

Luncheon and Beard Scene

The same. Afternoon. Two weeks later

A portrait of Lucia now hangs on the wall L *of the arch replacing that of Mapp's mother*

As the Curtain *rises, Mapp is seated on the sofa twisting her gloves angrily and impatiently*

Grosvenor enters UR *and moves to the sofa*

Grosvenor Mrs Lucas says that she has not finished lunch, miss, and she will not be able to see you for quite a little while.

Mapp Nonsense. It's half-past two. She must have finished.

Grosvenor Mrs Lucas has guests for lunch, miss.

Mapp Yes, I know. Major Flint and Mrs Plaistow. Please tell Mrs Lucas I insist on seeing her. It's extremely urgent.

Grosvenor (*dubiously*) Well, I'll *tell* her, miss. (*She starts* UR)

Mapp (*rising*) Oh, Grosvenor. Just one moment. Has — does Major Flint come here often to meals?

Grosvenor I don't know about "often", miss.

Mapp Has he ever been here alone?

Grosvenor I really couldn't say, miss.

Mapp Of course you could say. You must have waited at table.

No answer from Grosvenor

Didn't you?

Grosvenor I think I'd better give Mrs Lucas your message, miss.

Mapp That means he has. Since this mysterious illness of Mr Pillson's, I suppose. What *is* the matter with Mr Pillson?

Grosvenor I really couldn't say, miss.

Mapp Hasn't Mrs Lucas told you? Hasn't *she* seen him?

Grosvenor I don't think so, miss.

Mapp I don't believe a word of any of it.

Grosvenor (*after a moment*) Is that all, miss?
Mapp No! What's happened to my mother?
Grosvenor I beg your pardon, miss?
Mapp (*pointing to the portrait of Lucia on the wall*) My mother's portrait.
What's happened to it?
Grosvenor It's upstairs in the attic, miss.
Mapp (*coldly furious*) Go and tell Mrs Lucas that I'm waiting.
Grosvenor Very good, miss.

Grosvenor exits UR

Mapp looks at the Lucia portrait again

Lucia enters UR

Lucia (*over her shoulder as she enters*) Will you take in some more coffee,
please, Grosvenor? Now, Elizabeth, what is this? What is the meaning of
that insulting message you sent me? That you insist on seeing me?
Mapp I have something to say to you.
Lucia Obviously. What?
Mapp You may think I don't know what is going on behind my back, but
I do. I assure you I do.
Lucia What *are* you talking about?
Mapp This fête that you are proposing to give in my garden. Why was I not
asked to participate?
Lucia Because the Committee were informed that you had expressed
yourself as being strongly opposed to it, the moment you heard about it. It
seemed rather foolish, after that, to ask for your co-operation.
Mapp I never did any such thing.
Lucia Would you like me to call in Diva and Major Flint? They're lunching
here. They both heard you. In the greengrocer's. Apropos of which, if you
really do want to participate, you might care to supply the fruit for the
refreshment booth from your garden. It would be a generous gesture.
Mapp (*smiling sourly*) Yes, but I'm afraid I can't do that, dear. The fruit is
no longer mine to give. I've contracted to send my entire produce to the
greengrocer for the whole time you are here.
Lucia (*too sweetly*) Oh, *that*'s what you do with it. You sell it! Well, then,
perhaps you could let us have some fruit from Diva's garden. Or have you
sold *that*, too?
Mapp I will not send any fruit! The fête will not take place!
Lucia And what will stop it?
Mapp *I* shall stop it. This is *my* house ...
Lucia Not for another six weeks.

Mapp And I will not have all the ragtag and bobtail of Tilling swarming through my hall and my drawing-room, dirtying my carpets ——

Lucia There will be no admission to the house. I shall lock all the doors, or put up chains, and I'm sure no-one will be so ill-bred as to try and force them.

Mapp I won't have it. Do you hear? I won't have it!

Lucia Elizabeth, whether you will have it or not is a matter of the supremest indifference to me. The arrangements have been made, and I'm afraid *you* have nothing to say about them.

Mapp We'll see about that. I shall consult my solicitor.

Lucia Very well. But I think I should tell you that I have already consulted mine. And now, if you have finished, I would like to go back to my guests.

Mapp You may think that you can come in here and ride rough-shod over everyone. To say nothing of the scandal of your private life. But this isn't Riseholme, you know. Or perhaps it *is*. Perhaps *that*'s why you left there.

Lucia Elizabeth, I have no time to listen to your ravings.

Mapp There's some mystery about your leaving there, and I assure you that I am making it my business to find out what it was.

Lucia Goodbye, Elizabeth. Or shall we say, "Au reservoir"?

Mapp exits through the arch to L

Lucia goes UR *and opens the door*

(*Calling*) Why don't you bring your brandy into the drawing-room, Major? And bring a glass for me. (*She moves to the love-seat*) I think I could do with a little brandy now.

Diva enters UR, *carrying a dish of chocolates. The Major follows her, carrying a tray with a decanter of brandy, one glass half full of brandy, and one glass empty. He is smoking a cigar*

Diva (*eagerly*) Well, what did she want? (*She sits on the sofa*) What was it all about?

The Major puts the tray down on the side table by the armchair and pours a glass of brandy for Lucia

Lucia (*sitting on the love-seat*) Oh, just the fête. And why she hadn't been asked to help. I offered to call you both in to corroborate …

Diva I wish you had.

Major I'm glad you didn't. Put me in a very ticklish spot. After all, always been a friend of hers, you know.

Lucia Well, now, to get back to where we were when Miss Mapp interrupted us. *Will* you, Major Benjy?

Major (*giving Lucia a glass of brandy*) Now, I say, Mrs Lucas, I'd do anything to oblige you, you know that. And anything to help the hospital. But I draw the line at tableaux. Very glad to give my old talk on tiger hunting, what? Hang up a few skins in a tent to give local colour.

Lucia I'm afraid there wouldn't be time for *that*, Major. But just a couple of tableaux. We're so short of men in Tilling, and now, with Georgie ill and not able to be with us ——

Diva (*putting the chocolates on the sofa side table*) What *is* the matter with Mr Georgie? Lucia, you *must* know.

Lucia I don't. I just know he can't see anyone.

Diva Too mysterious, the whole thing. A fortnight now it is. Elizabeth's dying of curiosity. She's called there every day. So have I. But you can't get a word out of that parlour-maid of his. He doesn't (*lowering her voice*) — drink, does he?

Lucia No, of course he doesn't!

Major You know, there is one theory. Not my own, but — well, better not say where I got it from — no names, no packdrill, you know, but ——

Diva But what, Major?

Major (*sitting next to Diva*) Well, that thing he wears — on his head, you know. Wig, toupee, whatever it is.

Lucia (*indignant; in arms for Georgie*) Major Benjy, what *do* you mean?

Major Well, doesn't he? Isn't it? I mean, I don't know. *I* didn't say it was.

Lucia Who did?

Major No, no. No names, no packdrill. Sorry I spoke.

Diva But what did you *think*, Major?

Major Didn't think anything. Forget I said it.

Diva Well what did "no names, no packdrill" think?

Major Well, she — I mean, *they* — thought that if it had been a wig, he might have set fire to it or something — by accident, you know — and been keeping himself in hiding while they made him a new one, don't you know?

He and Diva laugh, then freeze as Lucia speaks

Lucia (*rising*) It's an absolute slander.

The Major rises

Georgie isn't well, and he wants to be left alone, and I think we should all respect his wishes.

Major Sorry, sorry. (*He puts his cigar out in the ashtray on the side table and pours himself another brandy*)

Diva (*rising and moving to Lucia*) Well, I must be going. Lovely lunch, Lucia. You know what's happening this afternoon, don't you?

Lucia No, what?

Diva The Hanging Committee's meeting for the Art Exhibition. You've sent in something, haven't you?

Lucia Yes, Georgie and I both have.

Diva I've sent in three, and I'm as nervous as a kitten. Awful disgrace if they turn you down. Still, I don't suppose *you*'ve anything to worry about. Well, au reservoir.

Diva exits through the arch to L

Major (*putting his glass on the tray on the side-table*) Well, I suppose I ——

Lucia No, don't you go, Major. Stay a little longer. I want to talk to you.

Major (*delighted*) Oh, really?

Lucia (*sitting on the sofa*) You know, Major Benjy, I'm very disappointed in you.

Major (*sitting next to Lucia*) 'Pon my soul, I'm sorry to hear that, Mrs Lucas.

Lucia Here I have all this responsibility, and Georgie ill and not able to help, and I turn to you, and what do I find? A broken reed.

Major Oh, don't say that, Mrs Lucas, please.

Lucia It's not much that I'm asking. Just for you to take part in two little tableaux. Sir Walter Raleigh — such a gallant figure — and Othello. Look, I'll make you an offer. I'll be your Desdemona, listening to your tales of adventure. Or, if you prefer, we can do the death scene, and you can smother me.

Major Oh, I say, I wouldn't dream of smothering a pretty woman like you, unless it was with — well, no, I suppose I shouldn't say what I was going to. (*He puts his hand on her knee*)

Lucia (*removing his hand*) No, I don't think you should. (*She rises*)

Major Sorry.

Lucia But what about it, Major? (*Lapsing into baby-talk*) Would oo do dat for me? Would oo play Otello if ickle me was your Desdemona?

Major By Jove, Mrs Lucas, there's one thing I've never been able to resist, and that's baby-talk from a pretty woman. (*He rises*) I'll do it.

Lucia Thank you, Major Benjy. You're a true knight-errant.

Major You know, Mrs Lucas, I don't see enough of you. Too many prying eyes around the place. That's the trouble. Why don't you and I run up to town, and have a little lunch there together one of these days?

Lucia That would be delightful, Major Benjy. Only I'm afraid the prying eyes watch the railway station, too, if they're the ones I think you mean. They live very close to it now, you know. In Diva's old house.

Major Got it in one, Mrs Lucas. But we could go up in separate compartments, on the train. Start in separate compartments, anyway. (*He steps towards her*)

Lucia (*evading him*) We'll see, Major. Vedremo, as we say in Italian.

Major You're a damn fine woman, you know. Don't know why you waste your time on that poodle-faking popinjay with the red ... (*Catching himself*) Steady, Benjy boy! Didn't say it, Mrs Lucas, didn't say it. Still, they tell me he does embroidery. That's not exactly manly, is it?

Lucia (*with great dignity and sweet reproof*) Major Benjy, Mr Pillson is my friend, and he embroiders for his nerves. Now run along. It's my hour for Dante. And remember, I'm counting on you. (*She extends her hand*)

Major (*shaking hands*) Can always count on Old Benjy Flint, Mrs Lucas. Well, a riverdoodlum.

He exits through the arch to L

Lucia (*to herself*) Oh, these men. These men! (*She picks up the Dante book from the sofa side table*) Dear Dante. (*She sits on love-seat, opens the Dante and reads soulfully*) "Nel mezzo del camnin di nostra vita." Beautiful, always beautiful. (*After a moment*) I wonder what it means!

Georgie appears at the french window. His face is covered by a scarf

Georgie Psst! Lucia!

Lucia (*rising*) Georgie!

Georgie (*in a loud stage whisper*) Draw the curtains.

Lucia What for?

Georgie (*as before*) I mustn't be seen.

Lucia Georgie, what is all this?

Georgie (*very agitated*) *Please* draw the curtains.

Lucia Very well. (*She puts the book on the desk and draws the curtains at the window during the following*)

While she is drawing the curtains, Georgie goes to the sofa, still holding the scarf over his face

Really, Georgie, what is all this mystery? You told me you had a little skin trouble.

Georgie lowers the scarf to reveal a beard, very grey in contrast to his red hair

Don't you think you're making rather a —— (*She turns and sees Georgie*) Georgie!

Georgie You see! Oh, my dear, it's been dreadful. Shingles. On my face and neck. Blisters and bandages. Too degrading. And the doctor says I shan't be able to shave for weeks. What am I to do?

Lucia (*after a second*) You'll have to play all bearded parts in the tableaux. Sir Walter Raleigh and Othello. You'll have to change with Major Benjy.

Georgie I wasn't talking about the beastly tableaux. I was talking about real life. I can't go around like this. I wouldn't have come out now, and let *you* see me, even, only I was so lonely I couldn't stand it any longer.

Lucia Ah, *poverino*. Let me look at you. (*She goes to Georgie*)

Georgie (*averting his head*) No.

Lucia (*turning him to her*) Now, Georgie, don't be silly. Let me look at you. (*She steps back*) You know, I think it's rather distinguished. Makes you look like a painting by Vandyck.

Georgie (*taking out a pocket mirror and looking into it*) Really? It wouldn't be so bad if it wasn't for its colour. There's not a grey hair in my head, and the stupid thing has come out like this. Do you think it could be because I'm run down?

Lucia I'm sure of it. You've only got to get stronger, and the colour will come right back. You see.

Georgie Yes, but till it does? What am I to do? If anyone sees it like this, they'll think I dye my hair.

Lucia (*very tentatively*) Well, then, I think I'd say — perhaps you'd better dye your beard.

Georgie Oh, I wouldn't like to do that.

Lucia Just a temporary measure. And, do you know, Georgie, I think it will be an improvement. The distinction, the dignity ——

Georgie (*looking into the mirror*) Really? Do you really think I could?

Lucia Of course you could. Drive over to Hastings and have it done there.

Georgie Well, as a matter of fact, I have got a little bottle of something at home. I've never told you, Lucia, but I do sometimes touch my hair up — just at the edges.

Lucia No?? I should never have suspected it. Although, as a matter of fact, Georgie, I think perhaps you should be just a little more careful how you *brush* it.

Georgie (*alarmed*) Oh, why?

Lucia (*very gently*) Well, just occasionally, the way it *lies*, makes it look as if — I know, you don't — but as if you might just possibly wear a toupee.

Georgie (*taking out a comb*) Oh, my goodness! No-one's *said* so, have they? (*He looks into the mirror and combs his hair*)

Lucia (*hastily*) No, no, of course not.

Georgie Why didn't you tell me before?

Lucia My dear, it didn't seem important. It's just a trick of the light sometimes, that's all. But *dyeing* it. That never occurred to me. You've done it beautifully. (*She sits on the sofa*) You'll have to show *me* how, when *my* time comes.

Georgie (*putting the comb and mirror in his pocket and sitting next to Lucia*) Oh, Lucia, you are so sweet. I have missed you so.

Lucia I've missed you, too, Georgie.

Georgie No-one to play the piano with. No-one to show my sketches to.

Lucia Poor Georgie.

Georgie I did get all my letters written, though. I've written to everyone in Riseholme. And who do you think has started a correspondence with Goosie and Piggy Antrobus, of all people? Mapp!

Lucia How do you know?

Georgie A letter from Goosie. I brought it with me. (*He gets a letter and glasses from his pocket*)

Lucia Mapp's been writing to them, you say?

Georgie Like mad, my dear, like mad. Here it is. (*He puts on his glasses, reading*) "Dearest Georgie, I should have answered your sweet letter before this, but so much has been happening. Whist drive, Church Bazaar ..." (*Taking off his glasses*) Oh, Goosie's mother has got a new hearing device.

Lucia No!

Georgie (*glasses on, reading*) "It's not an ear trumpet at all. She just bites on a small leather pad, and hears everything perfectly. Then she takes it out of her mouth, and answers you, and puts it back again to listen." (*Glasses off*)

Lucia All wet?

He puts his glasses on and refers to the letter, turns it over

Georgie She doesn't say.

Lucia Come to the part about Mapp.

Georgie (*reading*) "Who do you think has started writing to me? Your dear friend, Elizabeth." (*He breaks off*) I couldn't think who she meant for a minute. (*Reading*) "She seems to be fishing for an invitation to stay with us, which is a bit of a bore, but you know, Georgie, we're always delighted to do anything for a friend of yours and dear Lucia's."

Lucia (*bitterly*) Friend!

Georgie (*referring to the letter*) That's all there is about Mapp. Oh! And who do you think has taken a house there for the summer? In Riseholme, I mean?

Lucia (*nervously bracing herself*) I've no idea. Who?

Georgie The great Italian composer, Cortese.

Lucia, disturbed, rises

Goosie says he's composing a new opera. It's a blessing *we*'re not there. (*He puts letter away, removes his glasses and puts them away*)

Lucia (*with her back to him*) Why do you say that?

Georgie After the way we've gone on with our little bits of Italian, to go and meet a real live one? He'd only have to say two words to me in Italian, and I'd goggle at him like a mad goldfish.

Lucia (*turning, facing him*) Well, then, you should brush up on it. Work, as I do. I think I could hold my own, with Signor Cortese or anybody.

Grosvenor enters through the arch from R, carrying two packages, obviously pictures wrapped in brown paper and tied with string

Yes, Grosvenor, what is it?

Grosvenor A boy just left these, madam. The boy from the picture framer's, I think. One of them is for Mr Pillson. It's addressed to —— (*She turns and sees Georgie's beard*) Oh!

Lucia (*pointing to the love-seat*) Oh, yes! Put them down there, will you, Grosvenor.

Grosvenor Very good, madam. (*She puts the packages on the love-seat and starts for the arch*)

Georgie Oh, Grosvenor!

Grosvenor stops

Don't mention having seen me to anyone, please. Or say anything about *this*. I ... er ... I want to surprise people.

Grosvenor Very good, sir. It's — it's very becoming, if I may say so, sir.

Georgie Oh, thank you.

Grosvenor exits through the arch to R

(*Rising and going to the love-seat*) What the ...? Not from the Art Exhibition?

Lucia (*picking up one package from the love-seat*) It can't be.

Georgie (*picking up the other package from the love-seat*) I bet it is.

Lucia Hand me my scissors from the desk, will you?

Georgie gets the scissors and brings them to Lucia who takes them, cuts the string and opens her package. She hands the scissors to Georgie, who does same with his package and tosses the scissors on to the love-seat. With each picture is a typewritten rejection slip. The paper and string which covered the pictures is allowed to drop to the floor

Georgie (*reading his slip*) "Cordial thanks of the Hanging Committee ——"

Lucia (*reading her slip*) "But regrets that limited wall space ——"

Georgie Typewritten!

Lucia Yes.

Georgie Mapp's done it again!

Lucia But how? How? How did she get round the Wyses?

Georgie She's got them all in her pocket. And you said they needed us! They're all afraid of her, and I'm not surprised. Do you know, I believe it was she who gave me the shingles?

Lucia How could she? They're not catching, and she hasn't had them. (*She puts her picture and slip on the sofa*)

Georgie (*sitting on the love-seat*) No, but they're caused by nerves. Nervous upsets. The doctor said so. And mine started the day after her sale, when I found my Crooked Chimney in her sixpenny tray.

Lucia Oh, Georgie, you're too sensitivo. (*Going to Georgie*) Now you run home and dye your beard, and then come back and have dinner with me, and we'll talk it all over then.

Georgie (*putting his picture and slip on the love-seat*) It'll take some time to get the colour right. (*He rises*) Lucia, how are we going to face people? I bet *they*'ve all had their pictures accepted.

Lucia We'll face them with our heads high, Georgie. With our heads high. I don't deny that this is a blow but we must behave as if nothing had happened, especially with the Wyses. We must go on with the garden party and everything.

Georgie It's a campaign. A campaign to get rid of us. And she's winning it hands down. I may be sensitivo, but I know when I'm not wanted, and I know when I'm beaten, and that's more than you seem to.

Georgie covers his face with the scarf and exits huffily through the french window

Lucia rings the bell, then gathers up the string and paper from the floor and goes to the cabinet R of the arch

Grosvenor enters through the arch from R

Grosvenor You rang, madam?

Lucia Yes. Take this paper and string away, will you please, Grosvenor?

Grosvenor Yes, madam. (*She takes the paper and string from Lucia and starts for the arch*)

Lucia Oh, just a minute. You might take these, too, will you, Grosvenor?

She takes two of Mapp's pictures from the wall R of the arch and hands them to Grosvenor

Grosvenor These are the pictures Miss Mapp painted, aren't they, madam?
Lucia (*angrily*) Yes. You can put them in the attic with the other rubbish.
And you needn't bother to be careful with them.
Grosvenor Very good, madam.

Grosvenor exits through the arch to R

Lucia picks up Georgie's picture and rejection slip from the love-seat. Then she picks up her own picture and rejection slip from the sofa. She looks lovingly and heart-brokenly at the two paintings. Tears start; tears of disappointment and hurt pride. Sniffling audibly, she turns upstage to the cabinet, carrying the pictures with her

CURTAIN

SCENE 2

GARDEN PARTY SCENE

The same. Afternoon. Ten days later

A buffet table and bench have been set in front of the piano

As the CURTAIN *rises, the Major, dressed as Siegfried, stands* UC *looking at Georgie's "Crooked Chimney" picture and Lucia's picture, which are now on the wall* R *of the arch. He has a sandwich and a whisky and soda. Voices off* R *are singing "For They Are Jolly Good Fellows", followed by three "Hip-Hip Hoorays", led by the Vicar. During the song, the Major finishes his drink, goes to the buffet table, and pours himself another*

The cheers end, followed by applause from the crowd in the garden, and then Mapp enters through the french window. She carries a parasol

Mapp Well, that's over. Having a little refreshment after all your labours, Major?
Major Yes. Thirsty work, tableaux. Didn't expect to see *you* here today, Liz. Thought you wouldn't have anything to do with the fête.
Mapp I thought it was my duty to support the hospital.
Major Pretty good show, didn't you think?
Mapp (*putting her parasol on the piano, and pouring herself a Champagne Cup*) No, Major, I'm afraid I didn't. Oh, I admit that Lucia and Mr Georgie looked very gorgeous. Having their costumes specially designed, and made in London. Sheer ostentation. But the rest of you. Well, really! And you especially, Major. Being made an exhibition of like that.

Major What do you mean, exhibition?

Mapp Oh, Major, that costume, that wig. So unsuitable.

Major Oh, do you think so? Wig's a bit hot, I admit. (*He takes off his helmet with the wig attached*) But what's the matter with the costume?

Mapp No, I'm sorry. I shouldn't have said anything. I think it was fine of you not to mind when they laughed. But, as an old friend, I confess it hurt me to watch you.

Major Laughed? Who laughed? At *me*, do you mean?

Mapp Well, perhaps it wasn't at you. Perhaps it was at poor, dear Diva. (*She sits in the armchair*) I'm sure she looked just as silly as Brunhilde with that great shield over her bust, going up and down like a kettle lid every time she breathed.

Major Matter of fact, I wasn't supposed to be Siegfried at all. I was promised Sir Walter Raleigh and Othello, but that silly blighter went and grew a beard for them.

Mapp Well, naturally Mr Georgie would come first. Even if it meant your being made a convenience of.

Major Convenience? What do you mean, convenience?

Mapp Well, I couldn't help noticing that all the time he was ill, or supposed to be, she had *you* dancing attendance on her. I never like to see a man led by the nose by a woman. Especially when it's obvious he's only an understudy at best.

Major You mean, *me*? Understudy to that — tame cat?

Mapp Well, that's how it looked to *me*. And to one or two other people, too, I think. But if you don't mind — well, it *is* none of my business.

Major But I do mind. I mind a great deal. You're perfectly right. I *have* been made a convenience of. All she wanted was someone in case he couldn't show up. Then when he did, I could go hang for all she cared. (*With slow, painful realization*) I've been made use of! Dressing me up in these things! I shall go home and take them off at once! (*He puts his glass on the desk*)

Mapp (*rising, putting her glass on the buffet table, going to the Major*) Major, why don't you come and have some dinner with me this evening?

Major Well, we were all supposed to be having dinner here. The whole cast.

Mapp I've got some salmon. And perhaps afterwards, a game of cribbage just as we used to before — just as we used to?

Major By Jove, there's nothing I'd like better tonight than a good game of cribbage. And no Italian, eh?

Mapp Not a word. By the way, Major, do you still think *she* can talk it?

Major What? You've heard her often enough, haven't you?

Mapp I've heard her say *Giardino* and *Buon Giorno*, and a few more things like that, but I still wonder if that isn't really all she knows.

Major By Jove, I wonder if you're right!

Mapp I'm going away for the weekend, Major, and when I come back, I may have a little surprise for you on that score.

Major Oh? Where are you going?

Mapp That, Major, as our dear Lucia would say, is a *Segreto* for the *Momento*. There, you see, I'm almost as good as she is.

Major By the way, tomorrow's your big day, isn't it, Liz? Opening of the Art Exhibition. (*He points to the pictures on the wall* R *of the arch*) Are we going to see those things of yours that used to hang up here?

Mapp (*turning in angry surprise*) What??

Major Noticed they were missing. Two of theirs up there instead. So I thought ——

Mr Wyse and Mrs Wyse are heard off R

Oh, here they all come.

Mapp (*urgently*) Major, quickly, before Mr and Mrs Wyse come in. Take those pictures down, will you?

Major Why, what on earth ——?

Mapp (*frantically*) Please, Major. Please do as I ask. Take them down and hide them somewhere.

Mrs Wyse enters through the french window, dressed as Mary, Queen of Scots

Behind the sofa cushions or something.

The Major puts his helmet down on the cabinet R, *takes down the pictures, hides them under the cushion on upstage end of sofa, and sits on the sofa. Meanwhile, Mrs Wyse takes a sandwich from the buffet table*

Dearest Susan ——

Mr Wyse enters through the french window, dressed as Cardinal Richelieu, goes to the buffet table and takes a sandwich

Mr Wyse — How I congratulate you. Let me give you some Champagne Cup.

Mapp pours two glasses, gives them to Mrs Wyse, who passes one of them to Mr Wyse

Mrs Wyse Thank you, Elizabeth dear.

Mr Wyse I hardly expected to see you here today, Miss Mapp. I was told you didn't approve of our little endeavours.

Mapp Oh, no, no. On the contrary. Where are all the others?

Mr Wyse They've all gone home. All except us and our kind host and hostess.

Georgie, dressed as Sir Walter Raleigh, enters through the french window

Georgie Make way for Her Majesty, Queen Elizabeth! (*He goes* DR *and spreads his cloak on the floor*)

Lucia, dressed as Queen Elizabeth, enters through the french window and comes into the room, stepping on Georgie's cloak as she does so

Mr Wyse ⎱   ⎧ (*applauding*) Good Queen Bess!
Mrs Wyse ⎬ (*together*) ⎨ (*raising her cup*) Merrie England!
Major ⎰   ⎩ (*rising and getting his glass from the desk*) Cheers!
Mr Wyse Gloriana!
Georgie Glorious Gloriana! (*He giggles*)
Mapp (*curtsying*) Your Majesty!
Lucia (*taking Mapp's hand*) Why, Elizabeth, what a surprise. How nice of you to look in. *Ecco, le due Elisabethe.* (*To the others*) That means "The Two Elizabeths".
Mr Wyse Bravo — I mean brav*a*!
Mapp (*rising from her curtsy; surprisingly in bad Italian*) *Che bella habita. E che bella parucca.*
Lucia I beg your pardon?
Mapp Where did you get your *parucca*?
Lucia I don't quite ——
Mapp Oh, don't you know what that means? I'm sure Mr Georgie does.
Georgie What? What was it?
Mapp *Parucca.* Wig, Mr Georgie — *wig*!
Lucia (*in ultra-purist tones*) Oh, *parucca*! I couldn't understand your pronunciation. How clever of you to look all that up. And now, Georgie, get me a glass of champagne cup. I'm dying of thirst.
Georgie Of course. (*He tosses his cape on to the bench and gets two glasses of champagne cup*)
Lucia Dear Mr Wyse!
Mr Wyse (*by the armchair*) Why don't you come and sit down, Mrs Lucas?

Lucia sits in the armchair

You must be utterly exhausted after all your labours. (*Going to the sofa*) Let me bring you a cushion.
Mapp (*with a sharp cry*) Oh ...!
Lucia (*rising*) Why, Elizabeth, what's the matter?
Mapp Nothing, nothing. It's all right, Lucia dear.

Georgie You look quite white, Miss Mapp.

Mr Wyse (*finding the two pictures behind the sofa cushion and picking them up*) Why, what have we here? (*Reading the names on pictures*) "Pillson" — "Lucas" — These are very charming pieces of work.

Georgie Why, those are the two pictures that we sent to the Exhibition! They were hanging — (*he points to the wall* R *of the arch*) up there!

Lucia (*looking at the empty wall*) Yes, Mr Wyse. Surely you recognize them. They were both returned to us.

Mr Wyse But, Mrs Lucas, that is impossible. I am on the Hanging Committee. So are Susan and Miss Mapp. (*Showing the pictures to Mrs Wyse*) Susan, my dear, surely these little masterpieces never came before us?

Mrs Wyse Never. Never.

Mr Wyse (*slowly*) I'm afraid there has been some hanky-panky here.

Lucia (*looking at Mapp*) Perhaps *Miss Mapp* has some explanation.

Mapp No, I've no idea!

Mr Wyse When were these pictures returned to you, Mrs Lucas?

Lucia The day the Hanging Committee met, Mr Wyse. At half-past three in the afternoon.

Mrs Wyse But the Hanging Committee did not meet until four.

Mr Wyse Who delivered the pictures to you?

Georgie The boy from the framer's. I told the framer to send the pictures to Elizabeth direct, because she's the President. (*He looks at Mapp*) She must have sent him over to us.

Major You're not by any chance trying to suggest that Liz ——

Mr Wyse Were there any rejection slips with them?

Lucia (*firmly*) No, Mr Wyse. There were not.

Georgie (*astounded*) But ——

Lucia (*grabbing Georgie's arm*) Wait, wait! *I* see the mistake. It must have been the *framer* who misunderstood, and sent the pictures back to us, instead of to Elizabeth. Do you see, Georgie? (*Then to Mr Wyse*) So the Committee never saw them, and we imagined all the time, didn't we, Georgie, that you had simply rejected them.

Mr Wyse (*befogged*) But what were they doing, hiding behind that cushion?

Lucia (*after a second, almost triumphantly*) *I* put them there! Just now. Just before you came in. (*Looking at Mapp*) I slipped in here and took them off the wall and hid them there so that you should not be embarrassed by being reminded of them.

A gasp from Mr Wyse and Mrs Wyse

Mapp (*rushing into a torrent of relieved speech; sitting on the bench*) Oh, what a dreadful misunderstanding! Such a stupid errand boy! Stupid framer! What are we to do? The Exhibition opens tomorrow. Everything is hung. What *are* we to do, Mr Wyse?

Mr Wyse Well, *I* shall withdraw my paltry piece of Still Life …

Mapp (*rising*) Oh, no, that will never do. Withdraw that beautiful banana? No! Mine shall go. Two or three of mine. I insist on it.

Mr Wyse No, no, no! Let us not be hasty, even in self-sacrifice. I have a better plan. Let us put these two pictures on *easels*, by way of showing how deeply we appreciate our good fortune in being permitted them.

Mrs Wyse Yes!

Mapp Yes, yes!

Mr Wyse (*to Lucia*) If, indeed, we *are* permitted them?

Lucia If you really want them ——

Georgie It's extremely gratifying, but …

Mr Wyse Not another word. Come, Susan, my dear. (*He goes to the arch*)

Mrs Wyse (*shaking hands with Lucia*) So happy. (*Going to the arch*) So very, very happy.

Mrs Wyse exits through the arch to L

Mr Wyse Goodbye, Mrs Lucas. Until this evening. (*Then to Georgie, bowing*) Mr Pillson.

Mr Wyse exits through the arch to L

Mapp I must go, too, Lucia dear.

Lucia Are you sure you wouldn't like to stay and have a nice quiet talk?

Mapp Sweet of you, dear, but I want to go and have a word with that picture framer.

Lucia (*smiling*) Yes, I can understand that.

Mapp looks at the Major, than goes to the piano and picks up her parasol

Major I'll say goodbye, too, Mrs Lucas.

Lucia Goodbye, Major. And thank you so much. You were splendid. Everyone said so.

Major No need to use flattery now, Mrs Lucas. Not any more. Besides, it won't wash. I've had my eyes opened. I've been made a fool of.

Lucia Why, Major, what do you mean?

Mapp (*hastily*) Come along, Major Benjy. It's time we were going.

Major It's all right, Liz. No names, no packdrill. (*Back to Lucia*) But when you promise a fellow Sir Walter Raleigh and give him Siegfried, that's making a fool of him. I'm afraid I shall not be able to avail myself of your

kind invitation to dinner this evening. I have another engagement. (*He
turns to Mapp and then back to Lucia*) And as for that fishy business about
the pictures, I don't know what you were trying to insinuate, but I won't
believe a word against Elizabeth. She's the soul of honour. (*To Mapp*)
Ready, Liz? After you.

Mapp exits through the arch to L

The Major gets his helmet from the cabinet R *and puts it on*

Good-afternoon.

The Major exits through the arch to L

Lucia Well! She's got him back! (*She sits in the armchair*) Now, Georgie,
alone at last. I think I'll take off this ruff. It's been choking me for the last
hour. (*She takes off the ruff and hands it to Georgie*)
Georgie I've had something else choking *me*. I thought I should burst,
standing here waiting for them to go. She sent those pictures back on her
own, and I always suspected it.
Lucia Yes, so did I. But I never thought we'd have a chance to *prove* it.
Certainly not in front of everyone.
Georgie But you *didn't* prove it. You proved just the opposite!
Lucia Oh, do you think so? You don't suppose they *believed* all that, do you?
Georgie I stood here, rooted to the spot, waiting for you to rise and crush her.
Why on earth didn't you?
Lucia Because that would have been descending to her methods. (*Rising,
bringing two glasses of champagne cup and giving one to Georgie*) I'm
quite sure that they suspect the truth, and that they suspect that I suspect it,
and if they do, they must think me very, very generous. As for *her*, well,
I gave her some bad moments. I enjoyed that. And I've taken the moral
stuffing out of her far more completely than if I had denounced her. (*She
sips her drink*)
Georgie She hasn't any moral stuffing to take out. (*He tosses the ruff on to
the sofa and sips his drink*)
Lucia Well, then, I've put it into myself. In any case, I'd much rather hold
this over her for the rest of our time here. And I think, Georgie, it would be
a good idea if we were to keep those two rejection slips from the Hanging
Committee.
Georgie Oh, lord! I haven't got mine.
Lucia I have. I don't know what made me keep them, but I have an idea they
may come in useful — *still*.
Georgie (*admiringly*) Lucia, you ought to have been a general.

Lucia Well, let's start tidying up, shall we? (*She takes a plate and glass from the cabinet* R, *and puts them on the buffet table with her own glass*)
Georgie That's an idea.

Lucia starts to hum "After The Ball". Georgie picks up the hum with her as he places the napkin from the sofa in his belt, picks up a plate from the sofa and brings it C *with his own glass. As Lucia takes plate and glass from him, Georgie suddenly stops humming*

What was that sudden turn-about-face of Major Benjy's, by the way?
Lucia Yes, that was a little surprising, wasn't it? But I'm afraid, Georgie, that hell holds no fury like a *Major* scorned. (*She puts the plate and glass on the buffet table*)
Georgie (*getting another plate and glass from the desk and going back to her*) Scorned? Who scorned him? You mean, you did? You don't mean he was really sweet on you?
Lucia (*taking the plate and glass and putting them on the buffet table*) Well, that's rather a vulgar way of putting it. Though perhaps not quite so vulgar as the right way. He asked me to go up to town with him.
Georgie You mean, to — to ...?
Lucia I mean, to go up to town with him. I can't answer for what he had in his mind that we should do when we got there, but I could give a good guess.
Georgie The cad. The utter cad. But I always thought he was Mapp's special property.
Lucia (*smiling gaily*) Yes, so did she.
Georgie You didn't *encourage* him, did you?

Lucia's smile widens. Georgie backs a step

I believe you did!
Lucia Encourage him? Why, Georgie, you're not jealous, are you?
Georgie Jealous? Me? Of that — silly soldier man? I should hope not, indeed!
Lucia Then why do you mind? It isn't as though *we* — You and I have never thought of each other like that.
Georgie No, I know. But I don't like it.

Lucia laughs, teasingly

And I don't like the way you seem to be making a joke of it! (*With dignity, he gets his cape from the bench*) I shall go home now, and change and have a hot bath. (*Turning*) I'm not in the least jealous, but I think you're behaving very strangely.

Lucia laughs again. It infuriates him

Very strangely, indeed!

Georgie throws the napkin from his belt on to the buffet table and exits through the french window

Lucia (*amazed*) Well!

She stares after him in amused astonishment. Then she resumes humming "After The Ball" and turns up towards the arch to exit as ——

—— *the* CURTAIN *falls*

SCENE 3

MUSICALE SCENE

The same. Evening. A week later

As the CURTAIN *rises, Grosvenor takes the straight chair* R *of the cabinet to the front of the desk, exits through the arch to* L, *and returns with two gilt chairs, places one* UL *near the desk, and moves* R *with the other. As she reaches* C, *Diva is heard off* UL

Diva (*off* UL) Hallo, Lucia?

Diva enters through the arch from L

Oh, good-evening, Grosvenor. Mrs Lucas not about?
Grosvenor She's still dressing, madam. I think you're a little early. The concert isn't till nine.
Diva I know. I came early on purpose. I wanted to see her before it began. You go on with what you were doing.
Grosvenor (*placing the gilt chair* UL *by the piano*) I'll tell her you're here, madam. Is there anything I can get for you?
Diva Got any chocolates? (*She looks on the cabinet*)
Grosvenor I think there are some chocolates on the desk, madam.
Diva (*getting chocolate from the desk*) Oh, good. Need sugar. Good for the nerves. Got to sing tonight, you know. Oh, what did I do with my music? There, I forgot it. Left it at home. That shows you what a state I'm in. Now I'll have to go back for it. Well, good thing I came early. Don't bother to tell Mrs Lucas, then.

Grosvenor Very good, madam.

Grosvenor exits UR

Diva I'll take a couple of these to eat on the way. (*She gets chocolates from the desk*)

Georgie enters through the french window. He wears a blue velvet suit and carries two music books, pad and pencil

(*Turning and seeing Georgie*) Oh, hallo, Mr Georgie.
Georgie Hallo.
Diva Well, look at you! My, aren't you dressy!
Georgie Do you think it's too extreme?
Diva Extreme? I think it's sweet. I'd wear it myself if I had the figure. Did you design it yourself?
Georgie Sort of. It was my idea.
Diva Most of us *make* our own clothes down here, you know.
Georgie (*with an appraising glance at her gown*) Really? (*He puts the music books on the piano and makes notes on the pad*) You're a little early for the musicale, aren't you? Would you like me to go over your accompaniments with you?
Diva No, can't do that. Forgot my music. Came early to find out what the big surprise was.
Georgie Surprise?
Diva (*sitting on the pouffe*) Elizabeth's been telephoning all of us, telling us there'd be a big surprise here tonight. She's up to something. Wanted to be sure we'd all be here for it. Do you know what it is?
Georgie No, I haven't an idea. How very 'straordinario! But I thought Elizabeth was away.
Diva Came back this afternoon. Only went for the weekend. You don't know where she went *to*, do you?
Georgie (*nodding*) She went to Riseholme.
Diva What for?
Georgie She asked herself to stay with some friends of ours. Very peculiar.
Diva Probably wanted to gossip there about you two. Better write and warn them that they can't believe a word she says.
Georgie Oh, I think Lucia has seen to that. She wrote to them last week, and told them all about — things here.
Diva You'll be going back soon, won't you?
Georgie Yes, in four weeks. (*He makes more notes*)
Diva (*rising*) Must you? We shall miss you both. Why don't you stay on with us?
Georgie Oh, I don't think we could do that.

Diva I think I'll draw up a petition, and get everyone to sign it. I'm sure they all would.

Georgie (*putting the pad and pencil down, moving to Diva*) Why, do you mean — do you mean they *like* us here?

Diva But of course they do. Lucia's won everybody's heart. Oh, they like *you*, too. But it's so exciting, she and Elizabeth. Never know what's going to happen next! I think *Major Benjy's* gone off you both a bit, but ——

Georgie Oh, he's started cutting me. Just looks through me when I meet him, as though I was a cockroach, or something. It makes me livid.

A bell sounds off UL

Grosvenor crosses the arch from R *to* L

Diva Oh dear, there's the audience. And me without my music. Standing here gossiping. Well, I'll be back.

Georgie See you later. (*He makes notes as before*)

Diva exits through the arch to L *and is heard greeting the Major*

Diva (*off* UL) Oh, good-evening, Major Benjy.

Major (*off* UL *to Grosvenor*) Mrs Lucas at home?

During the following, Georgie, hearing the Major in the hall, puts down his pad and pencil and backs slowly towards the french window

Grosvenor (*off* UL) I don't think she's dressed yet, sir.

Major (*off* UL) Will you ask her if she can see Major Flint for a moment? Haven't come to her beastly musical evening. I'm not staying. But ask her if she can see me for a moment, will you?

Grosvenor (*off* UL) Yes, sir. Will you take a seat in the morning room?

Lucia enters through the arch from R

Lucia Georgie, I didn't know you were here. You heard who that was? Major Benjy. I wonder what he wants. I didn't think he'd set foot in this house again.

Grosvenor enters through the arch from L

Grosvenor Major Flint is here, madam. He wants to know if you can see him.

Lucia Yes, I heard. You'd better show him in.

Grosvenor I think, madam, I should tell you that I don't think he's — well, quite himself, madam.

Lucia I see. Well, show him in, all the same.
Grosvenor Very good, madam.

Grosvenor exits through the arch to L

Georgie Drunk! How disgusting! (*He pulls Lucia* R *a bit*) Lucia, I want to ask you something. Quickly. Did he ever say I wore a wig?
Lucia What? Georgie, what makes you think ——?
Georgie Something I've heard. Tell me, quickly, did he?
Lucia I think he — hinted it.
Georgie (*outraged*) I thought so.

Grosvenor enters through the arch from L

Grosvenor Major Flint, madam.

The Major enters somewhat drunkenly through the arch from L. *Grosvenor exits through the arch to* R

Lucia Good-evening, Major.
Major Evening, Mrs Lucas.

Georgie bows. The Major sneers, cuts him dead

Mrs Lucas, This is not a social call. Want to ask you a question. Just a simple question. You can answer yes or no. Then I'll make myself scarce.
Lucia Yes, Major, what is the question?
Major The question, Mrs Lucas, is this. Did you write to your friends in Riseholme about me?
Lucia I beg your pardon?
Major I said — did you write to your Rise-in-friendsholme about me?
Lucia I have written to my friends in Riseholme. I wrote them about this place, and the people here. I daresay I mentioned you.
Major Did you say that I had made improper advances to you?
Lucia (*moving to the piano*) Major Benjy, you are behaving very strangely. I don't care to be cross-questioned like this in my own drawing-room.
Major Sorry. Didn't mean to be ungentlemanly. But I've just been having a bit of an upset. Matter of fact, Liz came back this afternoon. Been spending the weekend in Riseholme. I went around to pay my respects and — well, as a matter of fact, she flew at me.
Lucia (*coldly*) Oh?
Major Wouldn't tell me why, at first. Then it all came out. It was on account of you. Of my having paid intention to you. Ordered me out of the house.

In front of some damned foreigner that she'd brought back with her. Fellow simply reeked of garlic. So I went home, and had a stiff whisky and soda, and I got to thinking. Struck me there was only one source it could have come from, and that was *you*. And I don't think it was a bit fair of you.

Georgie (*suddenly*) Why not?

Major I was not aware that I had addressed myself to *you*, sir.

Georgie No, you didn't. You didn't even say good-evening to me. You've been cutting me for days ... Ever since the fête here. Just because you wanted to play Sir Walter Raleigh and Othello, and I'm jolly sick of it.

The Major moves to Georgie who backs away

Major I would like to know, sir, just what you mean by those remarks. Are you insinuating that I would allow petty jealousy ——

Georgie advances as the Major moves back again

Georgie Yes, of course you would. You're as jealous as anything. And so is Elizabeth. Suppose Lucia did write that to Riseholme. It was true, wasn't it? You did ask her to go up to town with you, and that was lecherous in the extreme.

Major Sir!

Georgie Oh, stop calling me "sir"!

Major Would you prefer that I called you "madam"? (*He staggers* DL)

Georgie I shall ignore that remark. You're drunk.

Major Mr Pillson, this is something that cannot be continued in front of ladies. If you will step outside ——

Georgie I shall do no such thing.

Major Very well. Then my seconds will wait on you in the course of the morning. Good-night, Mrs Lucas. I consider your behaviour to have been most — most — I shall say no more.

The Major exits through the arch to L

Lucia Georgie, whatever possessed you?

Georgie I saw red. *Bright* red.

Lucia I've never known you to do a thing like that before.

Georgie Well, I just couldn't stick it. Standing there ignoring me. And then attacking you like that.

Lucia Georgie, that was very gallant of you. But I've never been so surprised. And to an old fire-eater like that, too. Why, it's like rounding on a tiger. (*She puts her hand on his arm*) Georgie, I'm proud of you.

Georgie (*backing away a little*) What did he mean by his seconds waiting on me in the morning?

Lucia (*amused*) I think he was challenging you to a duel.

Georgie Not seriously?

Lucia No, of course not. Nobody fights duels anymore. Besides, it's illegal.

Georgie Is it? Yes, but you said yourself he was a fire-eater. Suppose he does send seconds?

Lucia He was drunk.

Georgie Yes, but in *vino veritas*, you know. After all, I did insult him. And he's got a whole houseful of lethal weapons. Guns, and Indian clubs, and Assegais and things. Suppose he comes back with some of them. He might, you know. He might very easily.

Lucia Yes, I suppose he might, at that.

Georgie What am I going to do? I shall have to go away.

Lucia Where to?

Georgie I don't know. To London, I suppose. I'll have to. I shall go tonight.

Lucia You can't go tonight. There's no train. Not till six in the morning.

Georgie Can't I use your car?

Lucia It's Cadman's night off. He's taken Foljambe for a drive.

Georgie Oh, dear. Well, then, I shall catch the morning train. The six o'clock.

Lucia Georgie, it's ridiculous. If you really feel like that, you'd better apologize to him.

Georgie No. I've got some pride. (*Moving to Lucia*) I've *got* to go, Lucia.

Lucia What about my party?

Georgie I can't help your party. I couldn't play a note tonight. Or listen to one, either. Will you make up some excuse? I'd rather you didn't tell people.

Lucia (*gently*) I won't tell them.

Georgie moves to the french window

Georgie (*turning to her*) I'll write to you.

Georgie exits through the french window

Lucia goes to the piano

Grosvenor enters UR

Grosvenor Excuse me, madam. Miss Mapp just telephoned.

Lucia Oh? What did she want?

Grosvenor She asked me to say, madam, that she would be coming to your musical evening tonight, and that she would be bringing a gentleman with her.

Lucia How odd. Did she say who?

Grosvenor No, madam. She just said a gentleman.
Lucia I see. Thank you, Grosvenor.
Grosvenor Very good, madam. (*She straightens the music on the piano and starts to leave*)
Lucia (*suddenly*) Garlic!
Grosvenor I beg your pardon, madam? Did you say "garlic"?
Lucia Oh, my God! It's Signor Cortese!
Grosvenor Is anything wrong, madam?
Lucia No, no, it's all right. Grosvenor, run upstairs to my bedroom, will you? And in the top shelf of the bookcase you'll find a little red paperbound book. An Italian phrase-book. Bring it here to me, will you?
Grosvenor Very good, madam.
Lucia As quick as you can.
Grosvenor Yes, madam.

Grosvenor exits UR

Lucia Cortese, the great composer! (*She curtsies towards the arch*) Maestro, un gran onore. Io sono tanto onorato — (*Correcting herself*) Onorata! (*Moving to the sofa*) Si prega di — What's the word for "sit down"? (*Moving to the piano*) Play the piano? Tonare il piano? Suonare il piano? Is it *il* piano? *La* piano? (*Growing frantic*) Oh, it's no good! Now keep calm! Keep calm. (*Moving to the arch, reciting to calm herself*) Nel mezzo del cammin di nostra vita — (*Screaming*) Grosvenor!!
Grosvenor (*off* R *of the arch*) Yes, madam.
Lucia Can't you find it?
Grosvenor (*off* R *of the arch*) Yes, madam. I'm just coming.
Lucia Well, hurry, hurry!

Grosvenor enters through the arch from R, *carrying the phrase-book*

Lucia snatches it from her

Thank you, Grosvenor.
Grosvenor Yes, madam.

Grosvenor exits through the arch to R

Lucia opens the book

Lucia (*reading*) "This cheque needs endorsing."

She flips the pages

(*Reading*) "There will be a battle of flowers this evening." Really!

She flips a page

(*Reading*) "I have caught a chill. I have a sore throat. How much ..."

An idea strikes her suddenly. She breaks into a delighted smile

Laryngitis! (*Reading feverishly*) "Ho mal de gola. Ho perduto la mia voce. Ho una laringite. Non posso parlare."

The bell sounds off UL. *Lucia hides the book under the music on the piano and repeats Italian phrases until Diva enters*

Diva enters through the arch from L. *She carries her music*

Diva (*shaking hands with Lucia*) Evening, Lucia.

Evie, the Vicar, Mr Wyse, and Mrs Wyse enter through the arch from L

Lucia now speaks in a whisper until the end of the scene

Lucia Diva.
Diva What's the matter? (*She puts the music on the piano and sits in the armchair*)
Lucia Lost my voice. (*Shaking hands with Evie*) Good-evening, Evie.
Evie What's the matter? Have you got a cold?
Lucia Laryngitis. Lost my voice.
Evie Shouldn't you be in bed?
Lucia No, it's all right. (*Shaking hands with the Vicar*) Good-evening, Vicar.
Vicar Eh, that's a sad sound ye're making there, Mistress Lucas. It'll be a wee frog ye've got, I'm thinking.
Lucia (*shaking hands with Mrs Wyse*) Susan, dear.
Mrs Wyse Oh, my dear Mrs Lucas, how very tragic. Why didn't you put us off?
Lucia Didn't want to do that.

Mrs Wyse sits in the desk chair. Lucia shakes hands with Mr Wyse

Good-evening, Mr Wyse.
Mr Wyse So sorry.
Diva Well, Lucia dear, what's the big surprise?

The bell sounds off UL

Lucia Surprise?

Vicar Ay, Mistress Mapp's been telephoning all of us, telling us there'll be a big surprise for us here tonight.

Grosvenor crosses the arch from R *to* L

Do you no ken what it is?

Mapp is heard off UL

Mapp (*off* UL) Good-evening, Grosvenor.

Evie		Here she is! (*She sits on the sofa*)
Vicar	(*together*)	Mistress Mapp!
Mr Wyse		Now we'll know what it is!
Mrs Wyse		Yes, indeed!

Mapp enters through the arch from L *and goes to Lucia. Grosvenor crosses through the arch from* L *to* R

Mapp Lucia! Sweet one! Just managed to get here. And so sweet of you to let me bring my guest, Signor Cortese.

Cortese enters through the arch from L

Mapp turns to Cortese

This is Mrs Lucas. (*To Lucia*) I've told him, darling, how beautifully you speak Italian, and he's so looking forward to talking to you.

Lucia (*curtsying to Cortese*) Maestro, un gran onore. (*To the others*) That means "Such an honour". (*Back to Cortese*) Pardoni, signor. Ho una laringite. Non posse parlare.

Cortese Oh, che infortunato. Ho moito aspettato il piacere de la nostra conversazione nel la lingua Italiana. Signoria Mappa me dice che lei parla italiano tanto bene.

Lucia (*blankly, not having understood one word*) Si. Si. (*To Mapp*) Elizabeth, dear — introductions, will you? My voice …

Mapp What's the matter with it?

Lucia Gone. Completely gone. Laryngitis.

Mapp Signor Cortese — Mr Wyse.

Mr Wyse Delighted.

Cortese Onore.

Mapp Mrs Wyse.

Mrs Wyse Charmed.

Cortese Piacere.

Mapp Mrs Bartlett.

Evie I'm sure.

Cortese Onore.

Mapp Mr Bartlett.

Vicar How do you do.

Cortese Piacere.

Mapp And Mrs Plaistow over here.

Cortese Onore.

Diva Doesn't the Signor speak any English?

Cortese But yes, I spik. I spik verra good. But Miss Mappa she say I must talk Italian with Mrs Lucas and her friend — her friend with the — (*He indicates a wig and looks the company over*) Where isa da friend?

Mapp (*going to Lucia*) Yes, where is Mr Georgie? Don't tell me *he*'s ill, too?

Lucia No, no. A sudden call to town. A matter of life and death.

Mapp You mean, he won't be here?

Lucia Afraid not.

Mr Wyse Are you making a long stay with us, Signor?

Cortese Pleasa?

Mapp Mr Wyse asked if you are staying long. No, Mr Wyse, only till ——

Cortese Only tilla tomorrow. I catcha de boat from Seaport ina de morning. Miss Mappa she meet me in Riseholme. She snappa me up.

Evie giggles. The others laugh. Cortese goes to Lucia

When I tell her I go to Seaport, she insist I spenda de night in her house and meetta de charming lady who spika de Italian, and giva de parties for Musica. She tella me Seaport four five mile from Tilling.

Diva Four or five? It's fifty!

Cortese Fifty? (*Turning to Mapp*) But *you* tell me ——

Mapp Don't worry. We won't let you miss the boat.

Mr Wyse You are going to the Continent from Seaport, if it's not being too inquisitive? To Italy, perhaps?

Cortese No, no. Notta to Italy. I go to Le Touquet. There is a Prima Donna there. I take her my new opera. I play it to her.

Lucia Your new opera? Have you the score with you? Aveca la musica con lei?

Cortese Si. Si. I have it.

Mapp Not *here*.

Cortese But yes, here. I have it in the pocket of my overcoat. You think I leave it in your house to be burgled?

Evie giggles. The others laugh

Lucia Signor, you wouldn't … you wouldn't play it for us?
Mapp Really, Lucia, the Signor is tired.
Cortese No is tired. What have I dona to makea me tired? I sit in de motor
car. I hear you talk. Tella me all de stories of everyone here. (*He taps his
nose knowingly*) I know everything about you all! I likea to play. I bringa
de music.

Cortese exits through the arch to L

Lucia bustles about, delightedly, getting the company seated

Lucia Diva!

Lucia leads Diva L *and seats her in straight chair near Mrs Wyse*

Mr Wyse!

Lucia indicates the gilt chair UL. *He sits. Evie rises*

Evie!

Lucia indicates the sofa. Evie sits again

Vicar!

Lucia indicates the sofa. The Vicar sits on the sofa

Elizabeth! (*She indicates the armchair* DR)
Mapp Really, Lucia, this is something of an imposition. If I had brought a
bootmaker with me, you wouldn't ask him to make you a pair of shoes,
would you?

Cortese enters through the arch from L, *carrying his opera score*

Lucia (*going to Cortese*) Signor, Miss Mapp says it's an imposition to ask
you to play.
Cortese Imposition? What is imposition?
Lucia She thinks you don't *want* to play.
Cortese But yes, I want. I likea to play.

Lucia smiles at Mapp

Only three thing I likea to do. To eat, to make love, and to play! (*He goes
to the piano and spreads his music on the rack*)

Lucia (*going to Mapp*) Elizabeth, here ...

Lucia seats her in the armchair DR. *Cortese runs a scale on keyboard*

And me — here! (*She moves the gilt chair* UR, *close to the piano and kneels on it, facing Cortese with an adoring gaze*)

Cortese removes his cuffs, puts them on the piano and raps for attention

Cortese Are you ready?
All but Mapp (*ad lib*) Yes, please — quite ready — (*etc.*)
Cortese The opera is "The Risea and the Falla of Lucretia Borgia."

Applause from all but Mapp

It taka four hours.
Diva (*with an anguished cry*) Oh!

Diva freezes as Cortese glares at her

Cortese There is no act interruption. You do not *move*! (*He bows to Lucia*) So — the overture. (*He sits and starts to play*)

For a moment Lucia's eyes close in ecstasy. Mapp sits staring front, gloomily. Then Lucia and Mapp turn and exchange glances. Lucia gives her a radiant and triumphant smile. Mapp forces a sickly smile in return. Then she resumes her former gloomy pose. Lucia turns back, radiant, to Cortese

CURTAIN

ACT III
SCENE 1

MORNING SCENE

The same. Morning. The next day

As the CURTAIN *rises, Lucia is seated at the desk, writing letters with a quill pen*

The bell sounds off UL

Grosvenor crosses through the arch from R *to* L. *Then Diva is heard off* UL

Diva (*off* UL) Morning, Grosvenor. Mrs Lucas at home?
Grosvenor (*off* UL) Yes, madam. Will you come in?
Lucia (*calling*) Is that Diva?
Diva (*off* UL) Yes, dear — *me.*

   Diva enters through the arch from L

   Grosvenor crosses through the arch from L *to* R

Lucia I thought I heard your voice. Good-morning, dear. I've just been writing to my friends in Riseholme. All about last night. What an experience! (*She rises and sits on the love-seat*)
Diva Don't know how you stood it. Almost two o'clock before we got to the food.
Lucia I was entranced.
Diva More than I was. Every bit of me went to sleep. Except me. I couldn't, for some reason. Voice has come back, I notice.
Lucia Yes, I gargled all night.
Diva Didn't have a very long night to gargle in. Seen Mr Georgie this morning?
Lucia Georgie? No, I told you he was called to town.
Diva Isn't he back yet?
Lucia He only went last night.
Diva This morning — on the six o'clock.
Lucia How do you know that?

Diva Elizabeth saw him. She was having early breakfast with Cortese, so he could catch his boat. Saw Mr Georgie going into the station carrying a portmanteau.

Lucia Well, then, if he left this morning, how do you suppose he could be back?

Diva Major Benjy's back.

Lucia What do you mean? Did Major Benjy go away, too? What for?

Diva Lucia, you don't mean to say that you don't know? You said last night it was a matter of life and death. I was sure you knew. So was Elizabeth.

Lucia Diva, what *are* you talking about?

Diva You *don't* know. Well, then, I'll tell you. (*She sits on the bench*)

Lucia Please do.

Diva Well, what a morning! Half-past seven, sleeping peacefully, who should come banging on my door, but Elizabeth. Well, five minutes after she'd seen Mr Georgie, she looked out of the window again, and whom should she see this time, also carrying a portmanteau, but Major Benjy! Catching the same train! So off she goes to Major Benjy's house, wakes up his man, goes into his study — he'd been writing late into the night, it seems — ransacks his waste-paper basket, and what do you think they find?

Lucia I've no idea. What?

Diva Wills.

Lucia What?

Diva Wills! Drafts and drafts of wills, leaving everything he owned to *her*.

Lucia Major Benjy — to Elizabeth?

Diva So *she* says. Haven't seen 'em, of course, though she says she kept a couple. And a letter telling her he'd challenged Mr Georgie to a duel and saying goodbye in case anything happened. So, of course, that explained everything. *That's* where they were bound for on the train.

Lucia Where?

Diva To fight the duel. Don't know *where*, exactly. Men keep those things secret.

Lucia And the portmanteaux? What were they for?

Diva For the pistols!

Lucia (*laughing*) Oh, Diva, what utter nonsense. Pistols in portmanteaux. (*She rises*) Besides, Georgie doesn't own any pistols. He'd be much too frightened.

Diva (*rising*) Then how did he manage to wound Major Benjy?

Lucia What??

Diva Yes! While Elizabeth was sobbing, *I* looked out of the window, and whom should I see but Major Benjy himself, letting himself into his house — with his arm in a sling! Elizabeth rushed out to him, but he wouldn't talk to her. Still, it was a relief to know that he was alive.

Lucia And you mean you think Georgie's back, too?

Diva Should think he must be. Unless Major Benjy's killed him. Never thought of that.

Lucia I shall go and telephone him. Will you excuse me?

Lucia exits UR

Evie is heard off UL

Evie (*off* UL) Hallo, Lucia? It's me, Evie Bartlett.

Evie enters through the arch from L

Oh, good-morning, Diva. Where's Lucia?

Diva She's just telephoning Mr Georgie to see if he's all right.

Evie How's her poor throat this morning?

Diva Cured. Completely cured. Says it was gargling. I don't believe that throat.

Evie Oh, why not?

Diva I don't believe anything that happened here last night. Why did Elizabeth bring Cortese here, and ask everyone to come?

Evie I don't know. To give us all a treat, I suppose.

Diva No! Do you know what I think? It was to make Lucia talk Italian, so we could all see she couldn't.

Evie But she could — couldn't she?

Diva How do I know? She hadn't any voice. And then Mr Georgie not being here, either. That's too much of a coincidence. Just not probable.

Lucia enters UR

Lucia Oh, Evie.

Diva Was he there?

Lucia Yes, he was there.

Diva All right? What happened?

Lucia He didn't say. He'd just got out of the bath. He was all wet.

Evie Was there *really* a duel, Lucia?

Lucia Diva says there was.

Evie Yes, so does Elizabeth. She's running round telling everyone — telling them the Major fought Mr Georgie about *her*.

Lucia What??

Evie Well, she didn't exactly *say* that, but she hinted it. The Vicar asked her if she knew what the duel was about, and she said her lips were sealed — and then blushed like a sunset. (*She giggles*)

Lucia Diva, do you know about this?

Diva Well, there was the letter, you know, and the wills. I heard her telling Mr Wyse about letters and documents too sacred to be produced.

Lucia How perfectly outrageous! It had nothing to do with Elizabeth.

Diva Why, do you know what it *was* about, then?

Lucia I don't want to discuss it, but one thing I can and will tell you. It was not about Elizabeth. Where is she now, do you know?

Evie She's having her morning coffee in the Tea Shoppe opposite. I just left her there.

Lucia rings the bell by the fireplace

Diva Lucia, what's it matter what Elizabeth says or does? Look, there was something I spoke to Mr Georgie about last night. Why don't you stay on here with us for a bit longer? Get Elizabeth to let you the house for another six months.

Evie Oh, yes, that would be wonderful!

Diva I'm sure she would. She tried to let it to Signor Cortese, but he's settling in Riseholme.

Lucia (*startled*) What's that?

Diva Said he was so pleased with his opera that he wrote there, he was going to buy the house he wrote it in. Now you'll have him for a neighbour. Be able to talk Italian all day long.

Lucia (*recovering herself*) How wonderful. Such a great artist. What a privilege.

Grosvenor enters through the arch from R

(*Going to Grosvenor*) Grosvenor, Miss Mapp is having coffee at the Tea Shoppe opposite. Will you run across and tell her that I would like to speak to her immediately?

Grosvenor Very good, madam.

Lucia Tell her it's extremely important.

Grosvenor Yes, madam.

Lucia And, hurry, Grosvenor!

Grosvenor Yes, madam!

Grosvenor exits through the arch to L

Lucia (*moving to the sofa*) And now, Evie — Diva. Do you happen to know where the Wyses are now?

Diva I think they're still doing their shopping.

Lucia I want you to go and find them, and bring them here as soon as possible.

Diva But what on earth for?

Lucia Never mind what for. You'll find out. Will you go, too, Evie? Bring
anyone else you see, but I particularly want the Wyses. Will you do that for
me?

Evie Yes, yes, of course we will. And you will think about staying with us,
won't you?

Lucia Yes, I'll think about it. (*Pushing Evie towards the arch*) Now you go
along.

Diva Come on, Evie. I'll take the High Street (*she starts the song*) and you'll
take the Low Street, and I'll find the Wyses afore ye.

*Diva shoves Evie ahead of her through the arch. Evie giggles as they both
exit through the arch to* L

Lucia gets a key from the mantel over the fireplace L, *unlocks the desk drawer,
takes out the two rejection slips, closes the desk drawer, and goes to the piano*

Grosvenor enters through the arch from L

Grosvenor Miss Mapp is just coming, madam.

Lucia Good. And I'm at home to anyone who calls, except Major Flint.

Grosvenor Yes, madam.

The bell sounds off UL

Lucia There she is. We've taught her to ring, anyway. Go and let her in,
Grosvenor.

Grosvenor Yes, madam.

Grosvenor exits through the arch to L

Lucia replaces the key on the fireplace mantel L. *Grosvenor is heard off* UL
talking to Mapp

(*Off* UL) Will you come in, miss?

Grosvenor enters through the arch from L

Miss Mapp, madam.

Mapp enters through the arch from L. *Grosvenor exits through the arch
to* R

Mapp Good-morning, Lucia. Grosvenor tells me you want to see me.

Lucia Yes, I do. Very much.

Mapp Your voice has come back, I notice.

Lucia Yes, completely.

Mapp What did you want to see me about?

Lucia About this absurd duel that's supposed to have taken place.

Mapp *Supposed* to?

Lucia You don't mean you believe in it, too, do you?

Mapp Of course I believe in it. I have proof positive.

Lucia Well … More important is the explanation you have been passing
around as to *why* the duel was fought.

Mapp I don't know what you mean.

Lucia Oh, I know you have said nothing definite, but you seem to have
managed to make everyone believe that it was on account of *you*. I want
you to correct that impression.

Mapp I shall do no such thing. The duel *was* fought about me.

Lucia It was never fought at all.

Mapp *What?*

Lucia Elizabeth, I have just talked to Georgie on the telephone. I haven't all
the details, but there was no duel.

Mapp Then what were they doing going off together on the train?

Lucia They were both running away.

Mapp I don't believe you. If that's so, how did Major Benjy's arm get hurt?

Lucia He sprained it, lifting his portmanteau when they got out at the next
station together. Georgie made a sling out of one of his scarves.

Mapp It's not true.

Lucia Of course it's true. They made up their quarrel on the train, delighted
to be able to, and had breakfast together in East Tilling.

Mapp Even if that were so, there was going to be a duel. Major Benjy
challenged him.

Lucia Yes, he challenged him when he was drunk. But you were not the
cause of their quarrel, and I will not have everyone in Tilling believing that
you were.

Mapp What was the cause?

Lucia *I* was.

Mapp *You?*

Lucia Yes. Major Benjy was being extremely rude to me, and Georgie, very
gallantly, leaped to my defence.

Mapp And who do you think is going to believe that story?

Lucia Nobody is going to be asked to believe it. I'm not like you. I have no
intention of publishing it. But I will not tolerate your giving the other
impression. So you will please contradict it, clearly and incontrovertibly.

Mapp (*moving towards the arch*) I think I must be going.

Lucia (*stopping her*) Elizabeth, if you do not do what I ask, I shall have to
take steps to make you.

Mapp What steps, pray?

Lucia I don't know whether you have forgotten the two paintings that were rejected by the Art Exhibition only last week? (*She goes to the desk*) I allowed people to think that they had been returned from the framer's by mistake. *You* know that they were returned with two rejection slips from the Hanging Committee. (*Turning, showing the slips*) *These* slips. (*She moves towards her, holding out the slips*)

Mapp backs away

If you do not make the retraction that I have asked for, I shall be forced to show these slips to Mr and Mrs Wyse, (*she goes to the desk and looks out the window* L) who are on their way over here now.

Mapp (*after a moment*) This is blackmail!

Lucia (*turning to her*) So it is. Well, that's something I never thought I would find myself doing.

Mapp moves slowly UR

Mapp (*after a pause*) What do you want me to say?

Lucia I want you to say that the stories that you have been spreading are completely untrue. And that you invented them deliberately out of vanity. If you do this, I will hand you back these slips to do what you like with. If not ——

Diva is heard off UL

Diva (*off* UL) Here we are, Lucia. Found the Wyses.

Lucia Come in. Come in.

Mr Wyse and Mrs Wyse enter through the arch from L, *followed by Diva*

Good-morning, Mr Wyse. Good-morning, Susan.

Mr Wyse Mrs Lucas, so very delighted to learn that your indisposition has left you. (*To Mrs Wyse*) Susan, do you notice — the voice has completely returned?

Mrs Wyse I am so pleased.

Mr Wyse (*to Lucia*) Such a treat you gave us last night. Words cannot express ——

Lucia I'm so glad you enjoyed it. (*She goes and leads Mapp a step down into view of the others*) But it's Miss Mapp whom you have to thank for it, really.

Mr Wyse Ah, Miss Mapp, I did not see you standing over there.

Mrs Wyse sits on the love-seat

Lucia I think Miss Mapp has something that she wants to say to us.

Diva sits on the pouffe

Mr Wyse Yes?
Mapp (*moving to the bench*) No, no! I haven't anything to say.
Lucia Are you sure, Elizabeth?
Mapp Yes, I'm quite sure.
Lucia (*behind the bench*) Oh, well, in that case, *I* have. Mr Wyse, I don't know if you remember ——
Mapp (*moving behind the armchair*) No, wait a minute! Perhaps there is a *little* something.
Lucia (*sweetly*) Yes?

Evie is heard off UL

Evie (*off* UL) Lucia, I couldn't find the Wyses. Got the vicar.
Lucia I think, Elizabeth, we might wait for the vicar, don't you?

Evie and the Vicar enter through the arch from L

Good-morning, Vicar. You're just in time. Elizabeth has something she wants to tell us all.
Vicar Has she, now? And what might that be?
Lucia Tell us, Elizabeth. We're all ears.
Mapp Well, you all know about this duel that took place this morning ——
Vicar Ay, a most unchristian practice. I have it in mind to preach a wee sermon ——
Lucia Yes, Vicar, but let us not interrupt Elizabeth. Go on, dear.
Mapp I think you have heard certain explanations of it in which I myself was involved. Explanations that I'm afraid I rather — fostered.
Lucia (*waving the rejection slips as an encouragement to her to continue*) Yes?
Mapp Those explanations were not true.

Ad libs of astonishment from all but Lucia

I was not the cause of the duel.

The CURTAIN *starts to fall slowly as Mapp speaks*

It was not fought about *me*. There's no need for me to tell you who — I mean *what* — it was fought about, but it was not *me*.

Before the last words are out ——

Curtain

Scene 2

Evening Scene

The same. Evening. The same day

As the Curtain *rises, Lucia is seated on the sofa, and Georgie is seated on the pouff. Each has a demi-tasse cup of coffee*

Lucia It was a bitter cup for her, Georgie, but she drank it to the dregs. I'll say that for her. She drank it to the dregs.

Georgie Oh dear, I do wish I'd been there.

Lucia You couldn't have been, Georgie. It would have been most indelicate.

Georgie Yes, I do see that. And I do see that it was a triumph for you. But, you know, I'm a little surprised at your taking it all so seriously.

Lucia Georgie, after all these years I need hardly tell you that I'm very fond of you. And I'm certainly not going to have another woman claiming that your gallant gesture was made on *her* behalf.

Georgie (*rising*) My dear, how sweet of you.

He sits on the sofa and gives Lucia his cup, which she places on the side-table

I'm quite touched.

Lucia Yes. And now, Georgie, I've got something else to tell you. Something not so nice. That's why I waited until now, so as not to spoil your dinner.

Georgie Oh, my goodness, what's happened?

Lucia While you were having your nap this afternoon, Foljambe came to see me. She brought Cadman with her.

Georgie Why? You don't mean ...? Oh, my goodness, you don't mean that they're going to be married?

Lucia nods

When?

Lucia Just as soon as they can, without upsetting you, I think.

Georgie They can't get married at all without upsetting me. Oh, this is what comes of giving them the same night off. (*Rising*) I never thought Foljambe could be so selfish. And I'd just left her five hundred pounds in my will. (*He paces upstage*) The will I made last night. (*He paces downstage*) I left everything else to you.

Lucia Georgie, how sweet of you!

Georgie And this is how she repays it! (*Moving to the sofa*) I wonder — I wonder if we could work out something, when we get back to Riseholme. Have her come to me by day, and then go back at night to Cadman, if she wants to.

Lucia I expect she'd want to. But, Georgie, I'm afraid there may be an obstacle to that plan. You see, I don't think I'm going back to Riseholme.

Georgie What? Never? Lucia, why? Why ever not? (*He sits on the sofa*)

Lucia I've been thinking. In the three months I've been here, I've come to love Tilling. I don't want to say that Tilling has come to love *me*, but ——

Georgie Oh, but it has. Diva says it has.

Lucia Well, that would be very nice to think. But, in any case, I telephoned Riseholme this afternoon — to the Winters, my tenants there — and, well, they've offered to buy the house, so ——

Georgie Lucia, I've never heard of anything so dreadful. You mean, I'll have to go back there without either Foljambe *or* you?

Lucia Without either me or Foljambe, I'd prefer you to say.

Georgie What are you going to do? Stay on here? In this house?

Lucia Yes, perhaps, for a while. I gather she's anxious to let again. Then I can look for a house here to buy.

Georgie (*rising*) Lucia, I simply can't take this in. My whole world is crashing about me in ruins.

Lucia Oh, Georgie, it's not as bad as that.

Georgie It is. After we've always done everything together, to go back there without you — it'll be awful.

Lucia It won't be the same here, without *you*, Georgie. You wouldn't want to settle here, too, would you?

Georgie Me? Oh, my goodness, you mean — sell *my* house, and buy one here, too?

Lucia Why not?

Georgie Well, it's an idea. (*Moving to the love-seat*) It's rather a staggering idea. But I suppose, after all, I haven't really any ties. No *real* ties. (*He stops, looking at her*) Or — (*He makes a resolution, moving to the sofa*) Lucia, I know we thought we couldn't, but you don't think now that we could possibly — get *married*, do you?

Lucia Married?

Georgie Yes. Then we'd only need one house. And there'd be no trouble about Foljambe, either.

Lucia Those don't seem to me quite enough reasons for getting married.

Georgie Oh, I didn't mean *that*. I'd like to marry you, Lucia. You know, (*sitting on the sofa*) when you said just now that you were fond of me, I suddenly realized that no-one has ever said that to me before? In my whole life. And last night, when I thought I was going to be killed, I realized that I'm very fond of you, too.

Lucia Thank you, Georgie.

Georgie Of course, there are a lot of things we'd have to discuss, but if you would consider it ——

Lucia Yes, Georgie, I *will* consider it. I can't give you an answer now ——

Georgie Oh, I wouldn't expect that.

Lucia But I will consider it.

The bell sounds off UL

Visitors!

They rise. Lucia moves to the love-seat, Georgie moves DL

Well, perhaps it's just as well. I don't think we could go on talking with this hanging over us.

Grosvenor crosses through the arch from R *to* L

And, Georgie, no matter what I decide, I do thank you for asking me. It was very nice of you.

Mapp is heard off UL

Mapp (*off* UL) Is Mrs Lucas at home, Grosvenor?

Grosvenor (*off* UL) Yes, miss. Won't you come in?

Grosvenor enters through the arch from L

Miss Mapp and Major Flint, madam.

Mapp and the Major enter through the arch from L. *The Major is wearing his arm in a sling. Grosvenor exits through the arch to* R

Lucia Elizabeth!

Mapp Lucia, dear! (*She shakes hands with Lucia, then moves to the sofa*)

Lucia Major Benjy!

Major Good-evening! (*He shakes hands with Lucia, then moves to the sofa*)

Lucia How nice of you to call. Sit down, won't you? Georgie, ring for some coffee.

Georgie starts for the bell but is stopped by Mapp

Mapp We haven't time for that, dear. We have a round of calls to make. But we had to come here first. You had to be the first to know. (*She sits on the sofa*)

Lucia To know what?

Mapp Do you remember my telling you about that beautiful letter this dear boy wrote, and didn't have the courage to send me?

Lucia Yes?

Mapp Well — (*She turns to the Major*) Suppose *you* tell them, Benjy-boy.

Major Well, the fact is, Mrs Lucas, that Liz and I have decided to — er — well, "tie the knot" I think is as good a phrase as any.

Lucia Well, I do congratulate you.

Georgie So do I.

Mapp (*to Georgie*) Thank you. (*To Lucia*) Thank you, dear. I knew you'd be pleased.

Lucia Well, really, this is quite an epidemic. Or else *I* must have started a new fashion.

Mapp How do you mean, dear?

Lucia Georgie and I are getting married, too. Aren't we, Georgie?

Georgie (*astonished*) Oh — yes!

Mapp Oh — how wonderful. How lovely. Isn't it, Benjy-boy?

Major By Jove, yes, girlie. Splendid news. (*He sits next to Mapp*)

Lucia (*sitting on the love-seat*) When is *your* wedding to be?

Mapp As soon as we can make our arrangements. Though it won't be really a wedding. Just a Registry Office, you know. And then a little honeymoon in Italy. We must ask Signor Cortese to recommend some quiet place. (*To Georgie*) I'm so sorry you didn't meet him. But you will, of course, now that he's settling in Riseholme. (*To Lucia*) How you will enjoy that, Lucia. Lovely musica. Lovely long talks in Italian.

Lucia Yes, but I don't think we're going back to Riseholme.

Mapp What?

Lucia No. Georgie and I were just saying that we don't think we can tear ourselves away from Tilling.

Mapp (*heavily, insincerely*) You mean — stay here for ever? Oh, what joy!

Lucia In fact, we were wondering if you'd care to let us this house, while we looked around for something we could *buy*.

Major By Jove, that's a coincidence, eh, Liz?

Lucia What is a coincidence, Major?

Major Well, Liz and I were having a little argument — (*taking Mapp's hand*)
weren't we, girlie? — about where we were going to live. Her house or
mine, I mean — and I think I finally persuaded her that it's the wife's duty
to follow her husband. Don't you agree, Mr Georgie?

Georgie Oh yes, rather.

He giggles, then freezes at a look from Lucia

Lucia So you want to sell this house?

Mapp Well, not *want*, but ...

Lucia Will you give us first refusal?

Mapp Well ...

Major I think we could do that, don't you, Liz?

Mapp Let's talk about that tomorrow. No sordid business dealings tonight.
And now, heart of mine, we must be off on our rounds. So many calls to
make. To spread the glad tidings. (*She rises*)

Lucia and the Major rise

(*To Lucia*) Oh, by the way, who knows about you two?

Lucia Well, actually, no-one, yet. We were rather planning to keep it a secret
for a little. But if you want to tell people, I don't think we'd have any
objection.

Mapp I think keeping it a secret is a much better idea. Well, goodbye, Lucia
dear. I think we might — *kiss*, don't you?

Lucia I think — just this once.

They kiss. Mapp moves to the arch

Major (*shaking hands with Georgie*) Well, so long, Pillson, old man. All my
congratulations, and all that.

Georgie Oh, thank you, Major. And the same to you.

Major Pretty lucky couple of rascals, what?

He slaps Georgie on the chest. Georgie coughs

Mapp Come along, lamb-pie. We mustn't dawdle. (*She takes the Major's
arm. To the others*) Well, au reservoir.

Major Bye-bye.

The Major and Mapp exit through the arch to L

Lucia (*smiling at Georgie*) Well?

Georgie Lucia, did you mean it? Or was that just to spike her guns?
Lucia (*moving to the sofa*) Georgie, surely you can't think *that* of me? I
meant to say "yes" from the moment you asked me. I meant to say "yes"
tomorrow, but as she would never have believed we didn't do it just to copy
her, I decided not to wait.

She sits on the sofa and takes Georgie's hand. He sits next to her

Georgie You could have knocked me down with a feather. Will she sell us
the house, do you think?
Lucia Yes, of course she will. She'll make us pay through the nose, but she'll
sell. And now, Georgie, about all the things you said we'd have to discuss.
I think we're both very used to our privacy. I do think separate bedrooms
are essential, don't you?
Georgie (*tentatively*) Yes, but with connecting doors. After all, you're a
fascinating woman, Lucia. And if Major Benjy could think of taking you
up to town ... *well*!
Lucia Georgie, *did* that make you jealous?
Georgie Yes, it did. Nobody could have been more surprised than I was, but
it did. That's when I started thinking like this.
Lucia Well, it's very flattering ——
Georgie (*taking her hands*) Lucia — darling — you're lovely!
Lucia (*pleased and embarrassed*) Why, Georgie! (*She rises and moves* c)
About the wedding. I do rather feel that perhaps I owe it to Tilling to make
something of a splash. Especially since Elizabeth's is going to be so quiet.
Don't you? (*She sits on the love-seat*)
Georgie Oh, yes. I do think a proper wedding. It's so decorative. And the
music. Mendelssohn's "Wedding March" on the organ.
Lucia Oh, darling, not that. So lascivious, don't you think?
Georgie Well, Wagner's, then. I know you think he's vulgar, but — oh,
Lucia, this is going to be fun!
Lucia Dear Georgie!

*They sit and look at each other, Georgie giggling slightly and Lucia smiling
at him, until the silence becomes awkward*

Yes. Well, we can't just sit here grinning at each other like two Cheshire
cats. And we can't go on a round of calls like those two. (*She rises*) Why
don't we have a little musica? It's ages since we have. (*She moves to the
piano*)
Georgie (*rising, kneeling on the pouffe*) Lucia, tell me something. Did you
know Cortese was going to settle in Riseholme?
Lucia (*vaguely*) I believe Diva did mention something about it.

Georgie (*moving to the piano*) Is that why you decided not to go back there? That wasn't why you ran away in the first place, was it? Just because of *him*?

Lucia (*moving to the keyboard*) It may have had *something* to do with it. Perhaps, if we're going to be married, Georgie, I should tell you that I can't really talk much more Italian than you can.

Georgie My dear, I always knew that. (*Moving to the keyboard, removing his rings, and placing them on the piano*) And, Lucia, perhaps I ought to tell *you* something.

Lucia What's that?

Georgie (*touching his hair*) Well — some of this — is *not* my own.

Lucia Georgie, dear, I knew that, too.

They sigh and sit together at piano

Now — are you ready? Uno — due — tre!

They start to play the Wagner "Wedding March" as a duet. After a few bars, they kiss, as——

— *the* CURTAIN *falls*

FURNITURE AND PROPERTY LIST

ACT I
Scene 1

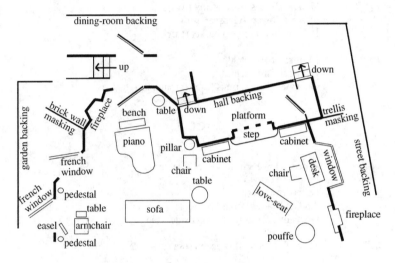

dining-room backing

up

down

brick wall masking

fireplace

bench   table   down   hall backing

platform

trellis masking

garden backing

piano

pillar   step   cabinet

step

cabinet

chair

cabinet

chair

window

desk

french window

table

street backing

french window

○ pedestal

table

sofa

love-seat

easel   armchair

■ ○ pedestal

fireplace

pouffe ○

On stage: 2 pedestals. *On them*: vases of summer flowers
Easel. *On it*: canvas
Fireplace UR. *On wall above*: flowered print
Bell pull
Round table. *On it*: urn of greenery
Built-in bookcase. *On shelves*: books
Piano. *On it*: Beethoven music book open, pile of sheet music,
   Lucia's glasses
Piano bench
Sofa. *On it*: 3 cushions (yellow on one side and brown on the other)
Round sofa table. *On it*: ashtray
Armchair
Small side table
2 cabinets. *In them*: books, bric-a-brac, etc.
Straight chair
Portrait of **Mapp**'s mother on wall L of the arch
2 pictures on wall L of arch
Desk. *On it*: pair of scissors, ink pot, quill pen, pile of unopened letters
   and postcards, notepaper and envelopes. *In drawer*: typed rejection
   slips

Desk chair
Fireplace DL. *On mantelpiece*: ornaments, geegaws, key to desk
    drawer. *On wall above*: flowered print
Love-seat. *On it*: copy of Dante's *Inferno*
Pouffe
Miniatures and other pictures on walls for dressing
Window curtains open
French windows open

Off stage: "Indian Diaries" manuscript (**Major**)
                Vase of flowers (**Grosvenor**)
                Parasol, full shopping basket (**Lucia**)

Personal: **Major**: wrist-watch
                Lucia: wrist-watch
                Georgie: glasses, rings (used throughout)

ACT I
Scene 2

Strike: Vase of flowers from sofa side table
                Easel and canvas
                Letters from desk
                "Indian Diaries" from love-seat
                Georgie's hat from armchair side table

Set: Vase of different flowers on sofa side table

Off stage: Section of door chain (**Lucia**)
                String shopping basket, half-eaten chocolate biscuit (**Diva**)
                Hearth brush, several curtain rings on a string, "Crooked Chimney"
                    picture (**Georgie**)
                Box of strawberries (**Major**)
                Tray holding decanter of sherry, 3 glasses (**Grosvenor**)

Personal: **Georgie**: handkerchief

ACT II
Scene 1

Strike: Portrait of **Mapp**'s mother from wall L of arch
                Vase of flowers from sofa side table
                Section of door chain from sofa side table
                Georgie's hat, curtain rings on string, "Crooked Chimney" picture
                    from piano
                Tray holding decanter of sherry from side table R

Set: Another vase of flowers of sofa side table
                Portrait of **Lucia** on wall L of arch

Off stage: Dish of chocolates (**Diva**)
                Tray with decanter of brandy, one glassful of brandy, one empty glass
                2 pictures (one "Crooked Chimney", one **Lucia**'s picture), with typed
                    rejection slips, wrapped in paper and string (**Grosvenor**)

Personal: **Major**: lighted cigar
                Georgie: pocket mirror, comb, letter, glasses

ACT II
SCENE 2

Re-set: Dish of chocolates on desk
                Armchair C
                Sofa in front of fireplace L
                Window curtains open

Strike: Armchair side-table
                Sofa side-table and contents
                Love-seat
                Brandy glass from piano
                Lucia's hat from piano

Set: "Crooked Chimney" picture and **Lucia**'s picture on wall R of arch
                Buffet table with plates of sandwiches, decanter of whisky, soda
                    syphon, jug of champagne cup, plates, glasses, napkins
                Plate on desk
                Plate and glass on cabinet R
                Plate and napkin on sofa
                Bench in front of piano

Check: Door UR closed

Personal: **Mapp**: parasol

ACT II
SCENE 3

Strike: Buffet table
                Ruff from sofa

Re-set: Bench to downstage
                Armchair to DL as before
                Pouffe in front of sofa
                Close curtains at window L and downstage french window

Off stage: 2 gilt chairs (**Grosvenor**)
                   2 music books, pad and pencil (**Georgie**)
                   Small phrase book (**Grosvenor**)
                   Music (**Diva**)
                   Opera score (**Cortese**)

ACT III
SCENE 1

Re-set: Window curtains open
                   Desk chair behind desk
                   Pouffe in front of sofa
                   Straight chair from desk to R of cabinet R as before

Strike: 2 gilt chairs

Set: Love seat as before

Check: **Lucia**'s glasses on piano

ACT III
SCENE 2

Re-set: Love-seat to C
                   Window curtains closed
                   Sofa on slant downstage of desk
                   Pouffe to L of love-seat

Set: Side table next to sofa
                   2 demi-tasse cups of coffee for **Lucia** and **Georgie**

LIGHTING PLOT

Practical fittings required: chandelier in hall, light brackets in recess, flanking fireplace L and above large bay window L

ACT I, SCENE 1. Morning

To open: Bright summer sunshine effect through windows

No cues

ACT I, SCENE 2. Morning

To open: Bright summer sunshine effect through windows

No cues

ACT II, SCENE 1. Afternoon

To open: Bright summer sunshine effect through windows

No cues

ACT II, SCENE 2. Afternoon

To open: Bright summer sunshine effect through windows

Cue 1   **Lucia** draws the curtains   (Page 33)
            Dim lighting L

ACT II, SCENE 3. Evening

To open: Practicals on; evening effect through windows

No cues

ACT III, Scene 1. Morning

To open: Bright summer sunshine effect through windows

No cues

ACT III, Scene 2. Evening

To open: Practicals on; evening effect through windows

No cues

EFFECTS PLOT

ACT I

Cue 1   At Curtain rise   (Page 2)
Bell off UL

Cue 2   **Grosvenor**: "I couldn't say, miss, I'm sure."   (Page 5)
Bell off UL

Cue 3   **Georgie** giggles   (Page 7)
Door closing off UL

Cue 4   **Lucia**: "Uno-due-tre!"   (Page 14)
Piano duet of second movement from Beethoven's
   Symphony No. 8

Cue 5   **Lucia**: " ... without ringing."   (Page 19)
Sound of front door being forced open and crash of broken
   chain

Cue 6   **Georgie**: " Besides, she's got sweetbreads for me."   (Page 25)
Bell off UL

ACT II

Cue 7   To open Scene 2   (Page 38)
Voices singing "For They Are Jolly Good Fellows",
   followed by three "Hip-Hip Hoorays", led by the **Vicar***,*
   and applause from crowd

Cue 8   **Goergie**: "It makes me livid."   (Page 48)
Bell off UL

Cue 9   **Lucia**: "*Non posso parlare.*"   (Page 53)
Bell off UL

Cue 10   **Diva**: " ... the big surprise?"   (Page 53)
Bell off UL

Cue 11   **Cortese** runs a scale on the keyboard   (Page 57)
Sound of piano scale

Cue 12   **Cortese** sits and starts to play   (Page 57)
             Piano music

ACT III

Cue 13   To open   (Page 58)
             Bell off UL

Cue 14   **Grosvenor**: "Yes, madam."   (Page 62)
             Bell off UL

Cue 15   **Lucia**: "But I will consider it."   (Page 68)
             Bell off UL

Cue 16   **Lucia**: "Uno — due — tre!"   (Page 72)
             Wagner's "Wedding March" piano duet